Breaking the Silence within the Church

"No one in church leadership wants to deal with moral failure or abuses. Too often leaders run the risk of doing more harm than good when they react to such situations. Ms De Wit has learned through multiple exposures to painful situations what dangers lurk when obeying Christ's mandate to care for our people. Learning from her may enable the reader to take the best road through this wilderness."

Rev. Nils C. Friberg, PhD, co-author with Dr Mark Laaser of *Before the Fall: Preventing Pastoral Sexual Misconduct.*

In *Breaking the Silence within the Church*, Judy De Wit provides coherent and complete use of Scripture and stories to demonstrate the causes and effects of abuse by church leaders, as well as the encounters necessary for congregational recovery. She clearly defines what constitutes abuse, and how it can occur, so that readers can clearly identify when it has happened in their own midst.

I especially appreciate the use of paradigms of parenting styles to understand the styles of church leadership. She compares the consequences of abuse and neglect in leadership by showing how they mirror such consequences in parenting. Just as abuse can occur within the family, it also can occur, systemically, in the church.

I find Judy De Wit's gentle approach in describing the needs of the victim particularly helpful in validating the experience of one who has been victimized. In guiding the church's structured response to abuse, she normalizes, and thereby gives some mastery of, the experience to the one who has been harmed.

The greatest benefit of this book, I believe, is that it provides a very practical course of action for the church to follow when dealing with reported incidents of abuse. Abuse is an emotionally charged event, but these steps are clear and objective. In following Judy De Wit's suggested guidelines, the church can avoid causing further harm to the victim and/or the accused. I believe this process can be redemptive and transformational for all involved.

I strongly recommend this book to Biblical Counselors, Christian mental health workers, and certainly to leaders of the church. It is a vital tool in addressing such a critical issue.

Melissa Baartman Mork, Psy.D.
Department of Psychology
Northwestern College
St. Paul, MN

Breaking the Silence within the Church

Responding to Abuse Allegations

Judy R. De Wit

iUniverse, Inc.
Bloomington

Breaking the Silence within the Church
Responding to Abuse Allegations

iUniverse books may be ordered through booksellers or by contacting:

iUniverse
1663 Liberty Drive
Bloomington, IN 47403
www.iuniverse.com
1-800-Authors (1-800-288-4677)

Because of the dynamic nature of the Internet, any Web addresses or links contained in this book may have changed since publication and may no longer be valid. The views expressed in this work are solely those of the author and do not necessarily reflect the views of the publisher, and the publisher hereby disclaims any responsibility for them.

ISBN: 978-1-4502-7059-5 (sc)
ISBN: 978-1-4502-7060-1 (ebook)

Printed in the United States of America

iUniverse rev. date: 12/20/2010

Contents

Acknowledgments   vii

Note from the Author   ix

Introduction   xi

Part 1   Identifying Abuse in the Church   xiii
    Voice of Bathsheba
Chapter 1   Where Does Abuse Come From?   1
Chapter 2   Parenting Styles and Personalities: 3
Chapter 3   Church Leadership Styles   16
Chapter 4   Abuse by the Church   21
Chapter 5   Avoiding Lawsuits by Ensuring Ethics   27

Part 2   Responding to Abuse in the Church   35
    Voice of Wesley Heersink
Chapter 6   Why We, the Church, Must Respond   39
Chapter 7   What Must Be Present in Responding   43
Chapter 8   How Does the Church Respond?   48

Part 3   Recovery from Abuse for the Church   61
    Voice of Nehemiah
Chapter 9   Recovery for the Betrayed Congregation   63

Part 4   Transformed Because Abuse Happened within the Church   73
    Voice of Jacob
Chapter 10 Why Victims Want to Meet   75
Chapter 11 The Transformational Journey   78

Part 5   Persistent for Justice   83
    Voice of the Persistent Widow
Chapter 12 Devote Yourselves to Prayer… and Then Watch   84

Bibliography   87

Endnotes   89

About the Author   91

Acknowledgments

Special thanks to these Brothers and Sister: Rev. Nils Friberg, Rev. Henry Gunnink, and Dr. Melissa Mork for reviewing this book and being an encouragement throughout the writing process. Revs. Bruce Adema, Jerry Dykstra, and Jerry Van Groningen, who were willing to take my endless letters, phone calls, and e-mails regarding abuse and abuse in the context of the church and who were found to have hearing ears and concerned hearts about abuse in the Christian Reformed Church.

To Brother Stan Heersink and to the Heersink families, who have been so courageous in their fight for justice for their Brother Wesley and who were willing to allow Wesley's story to be a part of this book.

To God, who I cannot thank enough—for it was He who took me through my own transformation in understanding abuse in the church and has granted me the needed peace I longed for.

Judy De Wit

Note from the Author

Abuse is a difficult subject to talk about, but we must.

It's difficult because the topic makes us feel uncomfortable and uneasy. Even as I wrote this book, I struggled with what to say and how to say it.

Abuse is about everything hurtful: shame, disrespect, disregard for another, using others, taking advantage of others, and the misuse of power. Abuse is about secrets, control, anger, and getting one's needs met no matter the cost. Abuse is about violating another's boundaries, creating distrust, and sending confusing messages about what relationships are suppose to look like. Abuse does so much damage.

There are different kinds of abuse: physical, sexual, emotional, verbal, spiritual, and church leadership abuse. Abuse comes into our lives in different ways, such as domestic violence, child abuse, sexual and physical assaults, spiritual abuse, dating violence, family violence, and abuse by church leaders.

My hope is that as churches struggle with how to respond when abuse occurs in the church, this book will provide a better understanding of abuse and where it comes from. Once we understand where it comes from, the better prepared we'll be to understand it and know what to do about it—in both our families and faith communities.

Judy De Wit

Introduction

The Christian Reformed Church, as well as other denominations, has struggled for many years to understand the topic of abuse, what it looks like, and how to respond to it.

In the mid-eighties and then into the nineties, the Catholic Church became inundated by sexual abuse allegations. Victims came forward and told stories of being sexually abused and assaulted by priests. What bishops had once covered up and swept under the rug now became exposed for all the world to hear. Victims demanded truth, apologies, restitution, and compensation as they shared how their lives had been destroyed by what the leaders of the Catholic Church had done. As the public watched and heard these victims' horrendous stories, Christians grieved and became enraged at the thought that church leaders could do such a thing.

At the same time, a similar thing happened in a church I know well. A woman from the congregation was hurt by her pastor soon after his arrival to the church. When the allegations against the pastor came forward, church leaders were quick to silence the abuse, call the victim a liar, and then allow the pastor to keep his position. The victim ran away amid the hurt of it all, and the church members were confused about what had happened. In the end, everyone lost.

Abuse in the church, by church leaders, must become a central concern for *all* Christians. Christ established the church to bring healing and grace to a hurting and broken world. He gave us the ministry of reconciliation. He never intended for His church to become a place of harm and destruction. Set apart and mandated, Christ's church is called to nurture and love others and to be a healing agent in a broken world.

The purpose of *Breaking the Silence within the Church* is to help churches, individuals, and boards or leaders know what to do if faced with allegations of abuse committed by a church leader against another adult. More specifically, this book will provide a council or elder board help in these ways:

- the ability to better identify abuse and where it comes from.
- a step-by-step process of what to do when abuse allegations come to the council table.
- a step-by-step process of how to help in the recovery process for your congregation in the aftermath of the abuse.
- methods for helping the victim and secondary victims come to a time and place of recovery, healing, and even reconciliation.

Too many times, I have witnessed or heard testimonies from councils who were unsure about how to proceed when allegations came forward. Fearing the worst, they responded with denial and/or avoidance in hopes that the issue would just go away.

(Note: This book does *not* address how to proceed when the allegations involve a minor. That process often requires a different approach simply because of the involvement of law enforcement and the church's need to cooperate with authorities.)

My prayer is that some of what this book presents will help you know what to say and do when allegations of abuse come to your council table.

Part 1
Identifying Abuse in the Church

Voice of Bathsheba

She was a beautiful woman. With her husband gone to war, her primary focus was the duties of managing a household. After completing her daily chores, she often took time for herself, which sometimes included bathing on the roof of her house. Her name was Bathsheba and she was the wife of Uriah the Hittite.

One day she was interrupted by a knock on the door. Men, sent by King David, asked her to come to the palace. She complied but was unsure what this request meant. Bathsheba went to see the king. After spending some time together, the king told her how beautiful she was. Then he said he wanted sexual relations with her. With no recourse of what to do or how to respond, she did as the king wanted.

A short time later, she discovered she was pregnant. With her husband gone to war, she knew who the father of her child was. Deeply distressed, she informed King David about the news.

When the news became known to the king, he moved quickly to make things look different than they were. But it didn't work. After being confronted by Nathan the prophet, the truth became known. King David was the father of Bathsheba's child.

So now Bathsheba was forced to face the reality of what had happened. She had been used to satisfy the desires of the king. Her marriage and life were ruined, and Uriah, her husband, had been killed by the man she was soon to marry. She was to enter a new marriage with a man she hardly knew, and God's judgment on David resulted in the loss of her son. There was little anyone could say or do that would bring comfort to her broken heart.

So it is with abuse of power. Whether the person in power is a king, a pastor, or a church leader, approaching leadership in a hurtful way victimizes innocent people, brings harm and destruction to many lives, and can be a demonstration of abuse and misuse of power.

The voice of Bathsheba cries out that power must be used to serve, not harm. The voice of Bathsheba reminds us that when deceit, lust, and sexual desires get in the way of proper leadership, people get hurt, their lives are destroyed, and their spiritual life and relationship with God are damaged.

Hear the voice of Bathsheba. Hear the voice of the abused. And answer that cry, and stop the abuse when it becomes known to you.

Chapter 1
Where Does Abuse Come From?

Train up a child in the way he should go,
And when he is old he will not turn from it.

Proverbs 22:6

It is a question many have asked: Where does abuse come from?

Does it come from generations of families whose parents abused their children and those children in turn grew up and abused their children? Does abuse come from living in and being a part of a frustrated, angry society? Does abuse come from a culture that says we are entitled to have anything and everything we want, no matter what it takes to get it? Are we mimicking the media, which shows that violence in our families and churches is okay?

I believe the answer to all of these questions is *yes*. Abuse is a product of all of these elements. What I want to present is a more in-depth understanding of how certain parenting styles and personalities can lend themselves to creating abuse or abusive tendencies. The challenge for you will be to look deeply within yourself and determine which style of parenting you experienced when you were growing up and how that style has formed the person you are today.

Looking back and analyzing your childhood is difficult. Admitting that you grew up in a dysfunctional family will mean being honest with yourself and owning what really happened during those years. Pride and fear will try to prevent you from being honest about your past. You might want to deny the bad things that happened and cling to the belief that you came from a "wonderful Christian family." Some denial of a negative past will come from the false belief that only those who lived on the "other side of the tracks" experienced abuse.

However, in your heart of hearts, you likely know that there were certain things while growing up that nobody dared talk about. Like an uncle who beat his wife, a bruised-up cousin, or maybe even your dad, who did bad things to your sister.

It's difficult to admit, but it's true: We all have been abused and we all have been abusive. So by gaining awareness about how your parents' style of parenting shaped and formed you, by making connections about how your childhood influenced you, and by piecing together how you became *you,* you'll better understand why you are the way you are and why you do the things you do.

And you'll begin to understand where abuse comes from.

Chapter 2
Parenting Styles and Personalities:

Rigid, Loose, or Flexible

May the words of my mouth and the meditation of my heart,
Be pleasing in your sight,
O Lord, my Rock and my Redeemer.

Proverbs 19:14

What follows is description of a continuum of two extreme parenting styles and/or personalities and the associated tendencies. It is important to understand that although abuse can occur on either end of the spectrum, abuse doesn't *always* happen. A person can come from a rigid parenting style and not have been abused. A person might also have experienced a loose style of parenting and not encounter abuse.

Imagine for a moment a continuum. On one end of the line is the word *rigid*; on the other end is the word *loose*. As these styles are described, determine where your parents were on that line when you were growing up (see diagram 2a). Dad and Mom might land in different places on the continuum. Follow that by determining where you think you and your spouse fit on that line. Compare and reflect why you put your parents, yourself, and your spouse where you did.

The goal of this activity is to help you understand what kind of upbringing you came from and how your childhood affected who you are today.

WHEN A RIGID PARENTING STYLE IS USED

Patricia (not her real name) came to my office with a somber face and tears dotting the edges of her eyes. She told me that she was having problems with anxiety and fear and that recent panic attacks were overwhelming her. She had come to counseling because she knew things weren't right but couldn't determine what the problem was.

After some time, Patricia began to share some of what had happened during her childhood. Her father was difficult to please, and nothing was ever good enough for him. She described him as harsh and stern and that he never had time for her. She was never to make a mistake, and if she did, she knew she would pay. This strict approach to parenting had driven her to get A's at school and to always check and double-check any task or activity to make sure it was correct. She often had to call her father to make sure that she was doing what he wanted.

As she remembered more about her dad, she couldn't recall him hugging her, encouraging her, or validating her. She couldn't remember him coming to many of her sporting events or concerts, and when he did, she remembers fearing what he would say. His criticism often resulted in a panic attack.

Her father used harsh punishments. Patricia could remember being beaten with a stick or electric cord and then isolating herself afterward by staying in her room for long periods of time. During her growing-up years, she had problems with sleeping and eating and often complained of headaches and stomachaches.

Now, as an adult, Patricia's fears and anxiety were continuing. She had taken a new job but was afraid she would make a mistake and be fired. At times she was unable to concentrate on her work, and at home she feared she wasn't doing things well enough to satisfy her husband. She admitted that her drive for perfectionism exhausted her, but she could find no other way to do things. Her cycle of "what if" thinking was constant, and when she made a mistake, she would beat herself up for being so dumb.

This rigid approach to parenting in this woman's life neglected the needed affirmation, encouragement, validation, and support she longed for. Patricia's emotional development was stunted; her need for things to be perfect dominated her life. The absence of her dad's acceptance and approval in her childhood resulted in excessive anxiety and fears in her adult life.

THE RIGID SIDE OF THE CONTINUUM

A rigid person, on the left end of the continuum, approaches relationships as:

- "my way or the highway"
- all about rules and obeying them
- all about structure
- a dictator approach
- being strict and harsh with others
- seeking to control everything about nearly everyone
- shame-based

Individuals who are rigid and controlling emphasize certain things. They focus heavily on thinking and doing with no time for feeling. They are constantly thinking about what needs to be done next and how it should be done, and they use harsh words to accomplish those things. Rigid individuals view feelings as senseless and foolish and would never think to ask their children, "How do you feel about that?"

Rigid individuals view love as conditional. Others must earn their love, which comes only through doing certain things. This means that even when tasks are done well, the rigid individual seldom offers a "Well done." Rigid individuals are incapable of affirming and encouraging others because of limited resources with which to validate.

Because children yearn to be affirmed and validated by their parents and because rigid parents are incapable of giving it, children of rigid parenting style are driven by an intense desire to be accepted and approved of by others. They start with Mom and Dad, but because rigid parents withhold validation and approval, these children end up looking for acceptance and approval from others. They may hope to hear it from their boss, their friends, or their peers. As these children age and mature, they become so desperate for approval and validation from others that they are driven to perform and do things in the hope of having their worth validated.

CHARACTERISTICS OF CONTROLLERS

Controllers, with their rigid approach to relationships, can be divided into two groups or levels. The first group of controllers is typically not as physically violent as the second group and displays control in more subtle ways. The second group is more intensive and obvious in the show of control. The first group is usually found in faith communities, and the second is found in family or domestic violence settings.

Controllers in the first group exhibit several traits:

- Controllers tell others how to think and feel. They use phrases such as, "You shouldn't feel that way," "You shouldn't be angry about that," and "Stop crying about that."
- Controllers undermine others' decisions. They call into question nearly everything a person does: "That'll never work…" "It's your fault. You hired the babysitter…"
- Controllers communicate shame. Family members are defective, lesser, or don't measure up.
- Controllers blame. It's always someone else's fault when things don't go well.
- Controllers use guilt. They make others feel guilty for not doing things the right way. They use phrases like, "You should have," "You could have," and, "Why didn't you?"
- Controllers correct others. They tell others where they are wrong. They believe they know what's best for everyone else and dictate to others how it should be.
- Controllers use anger. They yell, give the silent treatment, and name-call to get others to back down and submit.
- Controllers are reactive, defensive, and fearful.

Instead of responding to situations, controllers react.

Instead of hearing another's viewpoint, controllers become defensive because they feel attacked.

Driven by the fear of losing control, controllers become even more controlling.

The second group of controllers is more intense in their approach. Their controlling nature is more in line with what happens in abuse or domestic violence situations, as shown by the "Power and Control Wheel" produced by the Domestic Abuse Intervention Project.[1]

Along with the characteristics listed above, these five can be added:

- Controllers are jealous and possessive. They want all the attention from their spouse. They do not want to share their spouse with anyone and become suspicious and paranoid if he or she is gone for a while or spends time with friends.

- Controllers isolate family from extended family and friends.
- Controllers have power over money. Their spouse does not have access to household finances. The spouse must ask for money and is held accountable for every penny spent.
- Controllers threaten others. "I'll take the kids…" "I'll divorce you if you don't stop…"
- Controllers intimidate. When angered, they will punch holes in the wall, hold their spouse or child up against the wall, yell, throw things, and slam doors to make others back down.

CHARACTERISTICS OF CHILDREN WHO GREW UP WITH RIGID PARENTING

Growing up in a strict, harsh, "my way or the highway" environment is not good. Anxiety, perfectionism, shame, and obsessive-compulsive disorder are just a few of the effects.

Anxiety

When there is an ongoing fear that Dad or Mom might explode or rage, everyone experiences anxiety. In an attempt to avoid outbursts, the family enables—dodging this or that outburst—in hopes of keeping the peace. So many people have said to me, "We were always walking on eggshells—doing this or saying that, hoping Dad wouldn't explode." These family members trained themselves to ascertain what mood Dad was in: angry, frustrated, content, agitated. From there the family members would determine what the evening looked like: Dad's in a bad mood (we'd better run and hide) or Dad's in a good mood (this evening might go okay). Family members often try to appease, validate, or encourage Dad in an effort to keep the peace. Children of controlling and angry parents become very anxious adults.

Perfectionism/performance-based

Because of a parent's anger and rage, family members feel driven to do things well. Children of a performance- or approval-based approach to parenting want so much to do things perfectly because Dad demands it and gets upset otherwise. Performance-based parenting is similar to how a soldier is trained: bed made so perfectly that a coin can be bounced on it, footlocker be neat, clean, and orderly, and every bit of clothing pressed or polished to perfection. Similar expectations are the norm when rigid parents demand perfection from their kids.

Children in these homes grow up with excessive anxieties about things not being perfect—if something isn't perfect, they feel worthless. They have anxiety about getting A's in school, keeping their rooms clean, being liked or approved of by others, and dressing to look their best. Reaching their parents' expectations is all they know to be acceptable.

Shame-based

Shame is when we give messages to our children and others that they are defective, are lesser, and/or don't measure up. Shame says that a child's viewpoint has little value and that only certain viewpoints are acceptable. Parents who shame their children communicate that they don't have value or that their value is measured only by how much they can do and perform.[2]

Shame comes in two forms—good shame and bad shame. Good shame surfaces when we feel embarrassed or ashamed because we lied to our parents about where we were last night. Bad shame is different—it tells us that we are bad people, that we are worthless, that we have little value. Bad shame and its messages get at the very core of our personhood and do extensive harm to self-esteem and self-worth.

Guilt issues coexist with shame issues. Shame says, *I'm bad because of who I am,* while guilt says, *I'm bad because of what I do.* Like shame, guilt can be either good or bad. If I rob a bank and feel guilty, that is the good kind of guilt. If I choose to set a boundary with someone, say no when they ask for my help, and then feel guilty, that is bad guilt. Because bad shame teaches that it is wrong to make a fuss, to express an opinion, or to state one's thoughts and feelings, bad guilt easily surfaces for the person who has bad shame. This person often carries around loads of bad guilt, which causes much sadness and grief. A rigid parenting style often contains bad shame and bad guilt.

Obsessive-Compulsive Disorder (OCD)

The *Diagnostic and Statistical Manual of Mental Disorders 4th Edition* (DSM-IV) states that an obsessive-compulsive person:

> …has recurrent and persistent thoughts, impulses or images that are intrusive and inappropriate and cause marked anxiety or distress…as well as repetitive behaviors or mental acts so that the person feels driven to perform in response to an obsession…according to rigidly applied rules" (for more detailed description of OCD, see the DSM-IV).

Children of rigid parents often develop obsessive thoughts and compulsive behaviors. Obsessive thoughts are thoughts that keep repeating themselves. An adult who came from a rigid home can be obsessed about whether store charges are accurate, how best to wash dirty snow pants, or how orderly a bedroom should be. Because of these thoughts, behavior is driven to constantly check and recheck things to make sure it's right—to make sure it's "perfect." Rigid parenting has taught them that things need to be done a certain way.

Rebellion

Because of rigid parents' stringent expectations, their children often rebel. They rebel because they can't stand all those rules anymore. It's a way of getting back at their parents or showing them that the kids want some control over their lives. That rebellion can involve drug abuse or addiction, truancy, pregnancy, illegal activities, or running away. Sometimes the rebellion can be seen in smaller ways, such a chronic lying, sneaking out late at night, or poor grades.

False self

Because the demands of rigid parents, children learn that it's best to conform to what their parents want, including what they want them to be. To help keep the peace at the home, children put on a false self that complies with their parents' wishes and demands. This means the child has given up identifying and having his or her own thoughts and feelings about things and is taking on the parents' thoughts and feelings in order to satisfy the parents. It's a pretend and false way to show compliance with their parents. An example is when a child goes to college only because his parents want him to, not because he desires to. Eventually this person will have issues of depression and anxiety. These children live with a false self.

TYPES OF ABUSE THAT OCCUR WITH RIGID PARENTING

Physical, emotional, and verbal abuse are typically found on the rigid side of the continuum. Mark Laaser explains that this is where *emotional abandonment* occurs.[3] By not encouraging, validating, and affirming your children, by not hugging them and telling them that you love them, by not touching them appropriately or letting them share their thoughts and feelings, you stunt and confuse their emotional development. By the time these children reach adulthood, their emotions and feelings are ready to break through, as if through a tiny hole in a dam. This would be a good time for therapy.

Physical abuse typically includes hitting, slapping, punching, shoving, beating, throwing, burning, biting, or cutting. If a mark or injury has occurred, physical abuse has occurred. Other types of physical abuse include striking a child with a fist, shaking a young child, interfering with a child's breathing, threatening a child with a weapon, poisoning a child, or unreasonable confinement and restraint. Contact local Child Protective Services if you'd like more about the definition of *child physical abuse*. These kinds of child maltreatment are typically found on the rigid side of parenting and are reportable to the authorities or Child Protective Services.

Emotional abuse is more difficult to define or identify. Emotional abuse is the use of words, messages, body language, or anger in order to control. This abuse tears away at the recipient's self-esteem, self-worth, and self-confidence. False messages about who they are eventually lead to issues of depression, guilt, and despair. When parents tell their children that they are worthless, that they'll never amount to anything, or that the parents wish they'd never been born, emotional abuse has occurred.

Verbal abuse is more about the use of abusive words. It's similar to emotional abuse in that by using words, it makes the recipient feel worthless, lesser, even objectified. Shame is very much a part of verbal abuse. When words such as "When was the last time your head was examined?" or "You're just like your father" are said, verbal (and emotional) abuse has occurred.

WHEN A LOOSE PARENTING STYLE IS USED

Janet (not her real name) told me her story. She had gotten pregnant at sixteen and had a second child by eighteen. She admitted that she started drinking at age thirteen, and by the time she was fifteen, she was using marijuana on a daily basis. When she dropped out of school after her first baby, Janet's life changed dramatically—from partying and smoking pot to having to work to buy diapers and food for her child.

Now that she was married to her second child's husband, Janet was beginning to see the need to see a therapist and talk about her past. Her guilt over past mistakes was overwhelming, and yet she realized that her past could not be changed. Janet's desire was to find answers to these questions: *How did this all happen? How did I become the person I am?*

When I asked Janet about her past and about her childhood, she told me that her dad and mom were hardly ever around. They would sit at the bar every night and often came home after midnight. When Mom *was* home, she was often drunk, and Janet and her younger sisters had to fend for themselves. Often there wasn't any food in the house, and at one point, when she was six years old, Janet remembers being so hungry that she learned how to shoplift at the local corner store. She had been shoplifting ever since.

When her teen years came, Janet knew that her parents didn't care about her. She knew she could do anything she wanted and they would never check up on her. There were times when she wouldn't be home for days, but her parents never called looking for her. Dad and Mom didn't care.

In her early teen years, Janet became promiscuous. She remembers having sex with boys as young as age fourteen and experimenting with drugs and alcohol when with these young men. She went to school only occasionally and at times found herself in trouble with the law. Again, her parents never did anything about it. Dad and Mom didn't care.

This parenting style resulted in much confusion and chaos. Janet never experienced good boundaries and rules in her life. She didn't know what it meant to have consequences or punishment when she did wrong. She didn't know what accountability was. She didn't have it because her parents failed to give it to her. They failed to give her guidance, rules, expectations, and structure—all of which are necessary for healthy growth for children and teens. Janet's parents' chaotic approach to parenting led her to a chaotic way of life.

LOOSE SIDE OF THE CONTINUUM

The loose side of the parenting continuum can be described as:

- a "whatever" attitude
- no rules
- no structure
- anarchy
- permissiveness
- chaos
- shamelessness

When there aren't any rules, it really doesn't matter what happens. The loose side of the continuum says, *Do whatever you want. Do you want to do drugs? Be promiscuous? Steal, lie, cheat? Go ahead, because it doesn't really matter what you do.*

When my clients talk about their parents' loose parenting style, they often describe it this way:

> Dad and Mom never cared where we were or what we were doing. Mom never called to see where we were if we didn't come home at night. We would sleep several nights at friends' houses. They didn't care. They never called. We didn't matter to them.

SURVIVAL TECHNIQUES

When children don't have rules or expectations, when permissiveness and anarchy rule, life for children and teens becomes confusing and scary. There is no protection for them because there are no rules. Parents and others can do what they want to the children because there are no restrictions or limits. Dad can have sex with his daughter because there is no rule that says he can't. Children grow up afraid of not being safe.

Because loose parenting does not take time to nurture, protect, encourage, or help identify, children come to adulthood unsure of who they are. They have limited identity. They don't know who they are, what they can do, or where to go. So they turn to others in their search for identity. They cling to friends, dating partners, and sexual partners and search out welcoming social networks. Because they have never been taught about rules in relationships and have little sense of self, their approach to relationships is unhealthy. They have not learned to say no, set limits, or have respect for themselves and others because no adult has ever shown or taught them such a thing.

Adults who grow up in chaotic or loose households desire love and will do nearly anything to get it. One way is to demonstrate that they are willing to rescue the world. They overfunction in relationships, giving more of themselves than they should, and are driven to fix problems and people around them. They enable others to be dysfunctional because they live in the hope that the other person might accept them, validate them, and affirm them.

CHARACTERISTICS OF CHILDREN WHO GREW UP WITH LOOSE PARENTING

Adults who grew up in a home with loose parenting typically exhibit similar traits: They like to control and manipulate those around them; they interpret life experiences through a skewed lens that makes it say what they want it to say; they have abandonment and rejection issues; they have poor boundaries; and they usually suffer from post-traumatic stress disorder (PTSD).

Manipulation

In order to survive, these children learn how to make it. As they enter their adult years, their way of "making it" is about manipulation and working the system. In their childhood, they learned to fend for themselves and do things in a certain way in hopes of surviving. The same happens as they approach adult relationships. They try to get others to do what they want and often lie about or distort what happens around them.

Skewed perception

Adults of childhood sexual abuse learned to survive their childhood and also have a skewed perception of what is really going on around them. Their childhood taught them to read into things that aren't really there. They believe they are especially good at reading others' minds and interpret events to be what they want them to be.

Abandonment and rejection issues

Adults who came from the loose side of parenting feel easily threatened. They fear abandonment and worry that if someone were to leave them, life would end. These adults come nearly unglued if a relationship ends and will use manipulative approaches to restore the relationship. They interpret disagreeing with them as rejection, which triggers anxiety and fear. They worry that without others' approval and validation, they will be lost, can't continue the day—their lives are over. Suicidal issues often surface here.

Poor boundaries

Because no one has taught adults raised in a home with loose parenting about respecting boundaries, because their boundaries have not been respected, and because their experience has been that people can do whatever they want to each other, they have poor boundaries. They will say and do things that are inappropriate and become easily confused about what is about them and what is about others.

Post-traumatic stress disorder (PTSD)

Childhood sexual abuse often leaves a mark of trauma in a person's life (for full diagnosis of PTSD, see the DSM-IV). Trauma has triggers, which means certain occurrences today can cause the mind to jump back the fears from many months or years earlier. Those memories can be vivid, recurrent, intrusive, and real, as if it happened only yesterday, and can escalate anxiety to extremely high levels. Memories of sexual abuse or memories of not feeling safe will trigger the trauma and will leave the person feeling terrified of his or her environment. Because most of their growing-up years were spent with no rules or protection, these children feel unsafe and unprotected. They likely have PTSD.

False self

For those who come from a home with a loose style of parenting, they often conform themselves to what others want them to be. In order to be accepted by friends and peers, they show themselves to be whomever and whatever it takes to fit in.

SEXUAL ABUSE IS ON THE LOOSE END OF THE CONTINUUM

Because on the loose end of the continuum there are few rules and expectations and because anyone can do anything to another person without respect for the other, sexual abuse typically occurs here. Mark Laaser explains that this is an *invasive* approach to relationships: You invade on others and others invade on you without proper respect for one another. Because a father does not respect his daughter's right to privacy and protection and instead uses the daughter to meet his emotional needs, sexual abuse occurs. Or because conversations and interactions with one another are not properly filtered or screened, hostile relationships are created and there is a lack of regard for feelings and respect of others.

FLEXIBILITY: A HEALTHY APPROACH TO RELATIONSHIPS
WHERE *IS* THE HEALTHY PLACE ON THE CONTINUUM?

So far we have talked about being on either the rigid or the loose end of the continuum. Both have shown to be unhealthy approaches to relationships and to individuals. We need to land somewhere in the middle of the continuum—flexible.

To be flexible is to understand that our lives need rules, expectations, and structure but that at times we will need to bend and flex on those rules. When we're flexible we know about appropriate boundaries and use them. We value the importance of accepting one another and have tolerance and even respect for others' viewpoints. Being flexible means we can praise and encourage each other, validate each other, and realize that our feelings and emotions count. We're okay when things don't go our way.

11

Staying in the middle of the continuum is difficult. It doesn't come automatically or without thinking and effort. Being flexible means we *practice* things like give-and-take, having our way and then letting our spouse have theirs, and tolerating another's opinion while being able to disagree respectfully. Living in the middle of the continuum is about finding balance in our lives and in our relationships.

True self

People who come from a healthy family know who they really are. They have the courage to be who they *want* to be—to be themselves—and can express their thoughts and feelings in healthy ways. People with a true self can accept themselves for who they are. They are in touch with their thoughts and feelings and don't have to compromise to be liked or accepted. The *true self* is able to stand alone on issues and likes the self for who he/she really is.

A Healthy Flexible Family

We all know the difficulty of raising children in an environment that is healthy and strong. We are aware of the importance of rules and expectations, but we also know there are times when we need to bend those rules and expectations. A healthy parenting style might look like this:

The parent/parent relationship

In a flexible family, parents have mutual respect for one another. Each recognizes the strengths and weakness of the other, and both work to complement those areas with encouragement and understanding. Each strives to have tolerance for the other's mistakes, and both are okay with the other when they can't agree. There are efforts on both sides to compromise when needed, to give-and-take when interests vary, and to seek the other's interest before one's own.

The parent/child relationship

In a flexible family, parents work as a team in raising their children. They expect their children to obey and respect them. They hold their children accountable for inappropriate behavior and punish when necessary. Harsh and abusive punishments are never used. Flexible parents allow their children to express their opinions and feelings when done without defiance or manipulation. These parents have unconditional love for their children and view children as image-bearers of God. They help define their children's strengths and challenges and expect honesty and truthfulness from them. Flexible parents know how to ground their children and instill in them a structure that is necessary and crucial for their future. These parents realize the importance of flexing and bending rules when needed and believe that modeling appropriate behavior for their children is important.

The child/parent relationship

Children are expected to obey their parents and to show respect for them and others at all times. Children are encouraged to share their thoughts and opinions in good ways and are allowed to have differing viewpoints. They are contributing members of the family and are expected to do their part to help with family activities. Children can expect accountability and even punishment if their behavior is unacceptable.

FINDING BALANCE

The flexible family finds ways to work together. Parents use a balance of punishment and mercy, hard work and play, and time together and time alone. Flexible parenting allows family members to be respectfully honest with one other, protect each other when needed, and be quick to encourage rather than criticize. This parenting style sets proper boundaries, forgives, and values honesty, hard work, and integrity.

Being a flexible family is difficult! It doesn't just happen. But consciously working to use a flexible approach with your family increases the likelihood that your children will reach adulthood with a better understanding of who they are and why they do the things they do, and they will be more equipped to meet the challenges adulthood brings.

Parenting Style and/or Personality Continuum

Diagram 2a

Rigid	**Flexible**	**Loose**
Emotional abandonment (M. Laaser)		Invasive (M. Laaser)
Physical, emotional, verbal abuse		Sexual abuse
		promiscuous
X_____	_____X_____	_____X

Response: anxiety/perfectionism/shame/OCD/rebel

Description:

My way or the Highway	Give and take	Whatever
All rules	Believes in rules, but also times to bend on those rules	No rules
All structure	Appropriate boundaries	No structure
Dictator	Accepts others' opinions and viewpoints	Anarchy
Strict/harsh	Unconditional Love	Permissiveness
Controlling	Affirms and validates others	chaos
Shame- based	Praises, encourages, and nurtures	Shameless
	Has good understanding of feelings/emotions	

True Self: Being who you really are

Survivor characteristics:
little/ no identity
no sense of self
rescuer, enabler
codependent

Characteristics of Rigid:
Think and Do, don't feel
Conditional/unconditional love
Acceptance / approval issues
Shame and guilt

Characteristics of Loose:
manipulators
skewed perception/lies
abandonment/rejection
poor boundaries
PTSD

Controllers' characteristics:
1. tell others how to think and feel
2. undermine decisions
3. use shame, blame, and guilt
4. need to correct others
5. use anger – yelling, silent treatment, name-calling
6. are reactive/fearful/defensive
7. are possessive/jealous*
8. isolate others*

9. control money*

10. threaten others*

11. intimidate others*

False Self: Being what Mom and Dad wanted you to be

False self: Being what you think others want you to be

Characteristics of Children raised in rigid parenting

1. anxiety
2. perfectionism/performance-based
3. shame- based
4. Obsessive Compulsive Disorder
5. rebel

Created and compiled by: Judy De Wit, MA MA, LMFT

*Taken from "Power and Control Wheel," Domestic Abuse Intervention Programs www.theduluthmodel. org/pdf/PhyVio.pdf (accessed 27 June 2010).

Mark Laaser, Healing the Wounds of Sexual Addiction (Grand Rapids: Zondervan, 2004).

Chapter 3
Church Leadership Styles

We have different gifts… if it is leadership, let him govern diligently.

Romans 12: 6, 8

We have just looked at a continuum that shows what kinds of parenting styles abusers and victims might come from. Churches can also be seen through the lens of family systems.

Imagine a continuum on which the word *rigid*, at one end of the line, is changed to *legalism*, and the word *loose*, at the other end, is changed to *anarchy*. Let's explore these kinds of leadership styles—legalism and anarchy—to gain a better understanding of abuse in the church (see diagram 3a).

THE LEGALISTIC SIDE OF THE CONTINUUM

The Pharisees in the New Testament are a good example of a legalistic approach to leadership. They were constantly scheming and plotting ways to trick or snag Jesus. They were big into the Law. Perhaps one of their biggest criticisms of Jesus was that He broke nearly every law they made. They would say, "Don't carry your mat on Sunday," while Jesus commanded the one He had healed to carry his mat and walk. "No healing on the Sabbath," they'd say, while Jesus responded that some things are necessary to do, even on the Sabbath. Jews were not to associate or even talk with Samaritans. However, Jesus not only talked to them but also asked a Samaritan woman for a drink of water. In the Pharisees' minds, Jesus broke a lot of rules.

The Pharisees easily may have suffered from anxiety—about whether they were good enough, perfect enough, or obedient enough. Their fear of not measuring up drove them to work harder at making more laws and showing themselves and others that they must and could obey them. The Pharisees' performance-based approach caused them to pray in public places, to be "seen" wearing their tasseled garments, and to sit in the places of honor at banquets. They dealt harshly and critically with their people, looking down on them as lessers, and used their power to intimidate and control. Making others look bad and shameful calmed their own insecurities about whether they were good enough. The Pharisees' insistence that the Law be obeyed and punishment be administered when it was violated was about *the Pharisees'* attempts to make themselves feel better.

Remember when the Pharisees caught a woman in adultery and took her to Jesus, asking Him what should be done? His response was for the one who had committed no crime to throw the first stone (John 8:1–11). They must have felt angry and humiliated at Jesus' response; their law had been broken and Jesus wasn't supporting them.

This style and approach to leadership puts the Pharisees on the rigid (or legalistic) end of the continuum. Rigid Pharisees were only about law, legalism, and appearances. In Matthew 23, Jesus spoke out against the Pharisees: "Everything they do is done for men to see" (v. 5), and, "On the outside you appear to people as righteous, but on the inside you are full of hypocrisy and wickedness" (v. 28).

Your church leadership

Reflect on the leadership in the church you belong to, and think about whether it is similar to that of the Pharisees. Do they believe in a lot of rules? Do they put strict demands and expectations on congregants? Do the leaders tend to find ways to have *power over* you? Do they dictate what you should do, believe that things have to be a certain way, and then use shame, blame, and guilt to control you? Are they invested in appearances, becoming fearful and anxious when you don't comply with their demands? If so, your church leadership may be operating under a legalistic style.

Abuse by the church

Pastors and church leaders who use a legalistic/rigid approach to leadership run the high risk of being abusive to their church members. With heavy emphasis on doing things their way, pastors and church leaders may make themselves vulnerable to fall in the trap of using and abusing power, including control, intimidation, and threats. Their refusal to compromise on things, their closed-minded approach, and their negligence in standing for justice, mercy, and faithfulness (Matthew 23:3) causes them to forget the more important matters of the law. This style of leadership is about getting the leaders' needs met—such as approval, acceptance, and validation. Legalistic leadership becomes about power-centeredness and self-centeredness and not about God-centered, servantlike leadership.

THE ANARCHIC SIDE OF THE CONTINUUM

It may be difficult to imagine leadership styles in churches that struggle with being well-grounded in administration and government of laity, but it's a reality. In fact, it likely happens more often than one thinks. This would be the anarchic approach to church leadership.

Churches that have problems with sexual promiscuity among members, sexual permissiveness among elders and deacons, and homosexual leadership can be viewed as espousing an anarchic style of leadership. Leadership that fails to demonstrate self-control in one's personal life, fails to show self-discipline in both private and public lives, or fails to demonstrate a lifestyle aligned with God's requirements is operating under an anarchic approach to leadership.

As seen earlier, on the parenting style and personality continuum, church leaders who find themselves on the anarchic end of the continuum have trouble with appropriate sexual boundaries. Typically these problems stem from their own childhood sexual abuse issues. If you were sexually abused as a child, reestablishing healthy, appropriate boundaries in adult life is a constant challenge.

Sexual abuse by a church leader is usually found on the anarchic end of the continuum. However, any person or church leader can vacillate between legalistic and anarchic approaches. This means that a pastor can be rigid/legalistic in his leadership style when at council meetings or in dealing with church issues, while at other times show himself to be very loose/anarchic when it's about getting his own needs met.

In a church I know well, a pastor sexually abused a woman in the congregation within six weeks of him being there. Although in the council room and elsewhere he presented himself as someone with an ultraconservative Christian approach to the Bible and religion, he believed (and actually said) that "rules were made to be broken." With that in mind, he showed himself rigid/legalistic on one end and loose/anarchic on the other.

FLEXIBILITY: BEING WHERE JESUS IS

Neither end of the continuum is a good place for church leadership. Leadership for our churches cannot be rigid, based entirely on rules and laws. And it can't be loose either—whatever happens, happens. Church leaders need to find themselves in the middle, which I believe is where we find Jesus Christ Himself.

Church leaders need rules for our churches, and at the same time we must bend and flex on those rules as situations arise. Jesus believes in rules and the law. He spoke out against murder, lying, cheating, adultery, and idol worship. However when He confronts us about the sins we commit, He doesn't come to us in harsh and intimidating tones, threatening to abandon us, make us feel shameful, or cut us out of fellowship with Him. Instead He comes to us with reminders, accountability, sometimes punishment, and sometimes mercy as we work through the sins we have committed against Him. We ask Jesus to forgive us. He sees our remorse and forgives. We thank Him for this. Jesus demonstrates grace. Jesus is grace.

Abusive, legalistic church leaders like to have *power over us*. Loose, anarchic church leaders are *powerless*. Leadership in the middle of the continuum is about Christ having *power with us*. We have no power within ourselves, but with His Spirit, we move forward and do the work He desires. Our powerlessness becomes powerful because God is helping us. Him working through us and in us makes us able to accomplish more than we ever thought possible. Together, God and church leaders can lead His church to bring healing and restoration to a broken world. *Christ is about power with His people.*

Jesus talked with the woman at the well, whose race and lifestyle were unacceptable to the Jews. Her five previous husbands and current live-in must have been a disgusting representation of the Samaritan people, or sadly, an accurate depiction of that culture. But Jesus crossed the cultural barriers and did what Jews never did: He accepted her. Jesus did not approve of her choices—a promiscuous, adulterous life—nor did he condemn her for it. Instead, He found a way to confront her, accept her, and welcome her into His fellowship. Jesus invited her to partake of living water. And she accepted. The woman at the well was a changed person from that day on. Jesus' unconditional love was transformational.

Leadership in the church today needs to be the same. We are not commissioned by God to condemn anyone, to use our power to shame and ridicule others, or to love conditionally. Instead, by God's grace, we must strive for leadership in the church that finds the balance of confronting, encouraging, disciplining, and accepting, just as Jesus did.

The Church
Diagram 3a

| Rigid- Legalism | Jesus | Loose – Anarchy |
X	X	X
The Law	accountability	lawlessness
legalistic	value/identity	no rules
everything is about "do" and "appearances"	grace-based	live shameful lives
power over	power with	powerless
protect traditions – how we always do it	unconditional approval	no routines
ritualistic	unconditional love	no rituals
hierarchy	God's control	anarchy

Matt. 23:5
Everything they do is done for men to see.

Col 3:21
Fathers, do not embitter your children.

Matt 23:28
On the outside you appear to people as righteous but on the inside you are full of hypocrisy and wickedness.

Matt 23:23
You give a tenth . . but have neglected the more important matters of the law – justice, mercy, and faithfulness.

Matt. 23:13
You shut the kingdom of heaven in men's faces.

Prov. 16:29
A violent man leads one down a path that is not good.

II Tim 2:1
You, be strong in the grace that is in Christ Jesus

Pr. 22:6
Train a child in the way he should go.

Eph. 5:15
Be very careful, then how you live – Not as unwise, but as wise.

I Thess. 2:12
Live lives worthy of God.

Rom 8:6
The mind controlled by the Spirit is life and peace.

Prov. 16:21
The wise heart is called discerning and pleasant words promote instruction.

Jn 3:18
You have had five husbands, and the man you have now is not your husband.

I John 3:4
Sin is lawlessness

Luke 15:30
This son of yours squandered your property with prostitutes.

Pr. 13:5
The wicked bring shame and disgrace.

Col. 3:5
Put to death sexual immorality.

Pr. 10:23
A fool finds pleasure in evil conduct.

Created and compiled by: Judy De Wit, MA, MA, LMFT

Chapter 4
Abuse by the Church

"This is what the Sovereign LORD says:

Woe to the shepherds of Israel who only take care of themselves…! You have
not strengthened the weak or healed the sick or bound up the injured. You
have not brought back the strays or searched for the lost. You have ruled
them harshly and brutally…. I am against the shepherds and will hold them
accountable….

This is what the Sovereign LORD says:

I myself will search for my sheep and look after them…. I will rescue them
from all the places where they were scattered. I will bring them out from the
nations and gather them from the countries I will bring them into their own
land. I will pasture them on the mountains of Israel…. I will search for the lost
and bring back the strays. I will bind up the injured and strengthen the weak I
will shepherd the flock with justice."

Ezekiel 34:2, 4, 10–13, 16

Reminder: The discussion in this book refers to when an adult church leader abuses another adult.
Abuse of a minor deems a more complicated understanding and response because the church
must report child abuse to law enforcement and authorities.

PASTORS

The authors of *When a Congregation Is Betrayed* speak about how pastors have fiduciary relationship
and responsibility to their congregations.' What does this mean? It means that because of the
pastor's position, he has the responsibility to hold sacred trust in the relationship with his
congregants. Upon taking the position as pastor, he makes a trust with the entire congregation
that he is responsible to conduct himself in appropriate manners in relationship with the church

21

members as well as to conduct himself appropriately in any interaction outside the church. When he breaks that trust by violating a member of the congregation or even someone outside the church membership, trust between him and the church and between him and the entire congregation has been broken. Therefore, because it is his fiduciary duty to maintain appropriate boundaries in relationships with his congregation and community, he—not the victim—is at fault for the wrong that has occurred.

Marie Fortune says:

> I define clergy sexual abuse in the following way: Clergy sexual misconduct occurs whenever a member of the clergy engages in sexual behaviors with someone for whom he or she has spiritual responsibility.[5]

ELDERS AND DEACONS, PAID AND VOLUNTEER STAFF

The same standard for pastors could be applied to other leadership within the church as well. It is the expectations that elders and deacons, ministry leaders, Sunday school teachers, and youth directors will take the responsibility to serve and interact with church members appropriately. It is their responsibility to maintain appropriate boundaries and interact respectfully with congregants.

TYPES OF ABUSE WITHIN THE CHURCH

Just as there are different kinds of abuse in families and in society, so there are different types of abuse in the church.

Sexual abuse

Sexual abuse of another adult by a church leader can happen in a variety of ways and settings. Whether the church leader touches private areas, has intimate relations, or has sex with an adult in the church, sexual abuse has occurred. Note that this goes beyond adultery. It's much more than adultery because there is not equal power between the two parties. The pastor holds the higher power, and the victim has lesser power (and fewer resources). Therefore, it classifies as sexual abuse.[6]

Marie Fortune explains how sexual relations between a pastor and someone he serves or supervises is exploitive and abusive:[7]

- *Violation of role.* This is not what the pastor was hired to do. He was called by the church to serve in the best interests of others, not for meeting his needs.
- *Misuse of authority and power.* He has more resources in the relationship and must keep good boundaries to protect the congregant and himself.
- *Taking advantage of the vulnerable.* Someone who seeks counsel from a pastor is more vulnerable, meaning she has fewer resources to draw from than the pastor does. The pastor must ensure protection of the vulnerable in his work with the counselee.
- *Absence of meaningful consent.* Because there is an imbalance of power in the relationship, a victim's consent to sexual activity with the pastor does not excuse the pastor's responsibility to keep the relationship appropriate.

Physical, verbal, or emotional abuse

Anytime a church leader hits, punches, shoves, throws things, slaps, or otherwise hurts another person in the context of church leadership, physical abuse has occurred. Sometimes church leaders are known to verbally explode and rage. In their tirades, they may use ungodly language, throw things, or degrade others. Or a church leader may use intimidation or threats to get others to listen to him. This is called verbal or emotional abuse.

Emotional affair

When a church leader and a congregant engage themselves in long, intimate conversations about their personal affairs, desires, and wishes for one another, it's likely that an emotional affair has occurred. Kissing, touching each other, and intentionally meeting in certain places are evidence that things have gone too far. Text messaging, e-mails, and voicemails not related to church activity reflect that the relationship has crossed the line and boundaries are being violated. Again, the church leader holds the responsibility in the relationship to keep conversations and interactions appropriate.

Abuse of power (boundary violations)

All of the above are examples of boundary violations. Boundary violations in ministry involve church leaders going outside their area of work and responsibility and doing things they are not mandated to do. They may intrude into personal areas of others' lives in such a way as to control, manipulate, or unduly influence them. Remember, if a church leader comes from the legalistic end of the continuum, he entitles himself to violate boundaries. On the anarchy end of things, there is very little (or no) use of boundaries.

Examples of boundary violations can include a pastor's surprise drop-in on a woman who's home alone, excessive e-mailing and text messaging, meeting women in coffee shops and restaurants without good reason or witnesses, sharing private information with congregants, getting involved with members' finances, or demonstrating favoritism to certain members of the congregation.

Breaching confidentiality

It's a big challenge for church leaders to respect and keep private the confidential information that their members and others share. Pastors, church councils, ministry staff, denominational personnel, and classis leaders are all enticed to gossip, slander, and degrade one another. Knowing negative things about others and spreading it around to those who do not need to know sometimes demonstrates how much church leaders struggle with their own self-esteems. Breaching privileged and confidential communication and information, inside and outside of membership, is abusive and causes harm to innocent parties.

Defining some terms:

Privileged communication is defined as "statements and conversations made under circumstances of assured confidentiality which must not be disclosed in court."[8] So if the accused pastor admits to his colleague that he has had sexual relations with an adult congregant and the disclosure is considered privileged communication, the colleague is prohibited from reporting the information in court.

Confidential communication is defined as "certain written communication which can be kept confidential and need not be disclosed in court as evidence, answered by a witness either in depositions or trial, or provided to the parties to a lawsuit or their attorneys."[9] For example, if a pastor admits to sexual activity with a congregant in written communication to his attorney, that information cannot be used in court against him because it is confidential communication.

Disclosure of private information by congregants to pastors is assumed confidential and needs to be confidential to build trust in the relationship.[10] It's generally believed that a counselee who shares private information with the pastor can do so without fear of that information going public in any way. Any time disclosure of a congregant's private information by a pastor or church leader occurs without the counselee's knowledge or consent, confidentiality has been breached and harm is likely to have occurred. Legal ramifications can occur against the pastor in certain situations.

False allegations

Hearsay and gossip are the roots of a difficult problem in the Christian church. Spreading false allegations about others does great harm. Dictionary.com defines *slander*[11] as false statements used to defame someone. In the world of law, slander is verbal defamation rather than defamation by writing or pictures.

Dictionary.com defines *libel* as misrepresenting damagingly.[12] In law, libel is about the written word or pictures that defame another.

Whether via written letters or word of mouth, hearsay, gossip, and false allegations are slander and/or libel and can come under serious attacks in civil lawsuits. But even more important, Scripture says in Titus 3:2, "Slander no one."

Failure to use proper process

There is a purpose and reason for establishing guidelines and procedures when addressing grievances in the church. Although these guidelines are just that—guidelines—they were established and adopted with the understanding that their use would provide protection for the complainant and the accused. Failure to follow established guidelines increases the likelihood of more harm occurring. Whether a council or elder board dismisses a called pastor without using proper process, or an abuse response team does not do what they are mandated and trained to do, or a pastor takes things into his own hands instead of doing consultation with his council, hurt and abuse can occur.

Time factors are typically problems during the use of processes. Councils and elder boards need reminders that completing grievance or appeal processes in a timely manner ensures better outcomes for all.

Unethical behavior

Behavior that does not reflect proper conduct for a particular position or expectation is called unethical. If your doctor became enraged with you and threw his stethoscope against the wall, his behavior would be considered unethical, not something you'd expect from a professional.

Pastors and church leaders are under similar expectations. When their conduct and behavior does not reflect what you would consider proper for their offices, it would be called unethical. It is unethical for a pastor to come to work drunk, to cuss and swear publicly, or to degrade his staff and council. It is unethical for council members to make fun of and ridicule congregants of different color or race or for them to make rude or crude jokes about church members.

In the scope of the subject of abuse, it would be considered unethical for a pastor to kiss a woman, to flirt with someone, to hug excessively, or to send e-mails that talk about sex. I remember an instance where the pastor put candy in his pants' pockets and asked kids to reach into his pockets on Sunday to get it. Later, that same pastor was accused of sexual abusing children. In another instance, a pastor gave a neck rub to a woman in his study, and it turned out to be much more than just a neck rub. Later allegations of sexual abuse were brought against him.

Illegal activity

One might not think a pastor would get involved in illegal activity, but it has happened. In one instance, a pastor took text from books and used it in presentations without giving proper citations or credit to the authors. When confronted, he denied it—until someone revealed his lies by showing the original text he had copied.

In another situation, a pastor became so involved in gambling on the Internet that his credit cards were maxed out and he was left with no money to pay his bills. When confronted about missing money from the church, he admitted he had taken some of the church's money to cover gambling debts.

ABOUT PASTORS AND PORNOGRAPHY

Mark Laaser shares that studies have reported that 40 percent of all pastors have admitted to having a problem with pornography, 23 percent of three hundred questioned have done something sexually inappropriate with someone other than their spouse, and 12 percent have engaged in intercourse with someone other than their spouse.[13]

Sexual addicts, as Mark Laaser states, become engaged in three different levels of addiction.[14] The first is fantasizing about sex to an extreme level. You may not think anything sexual about the young woman on TV who looks good in a pink outfit. However, the person who fantasizes about sex excessively looks at the same woman and imagines what it would be like to go to bed with her. This is fantasizing about sex that far exceeds normal limits.

Next comes the use of pornography. Pornography provides images and ideas for a person to use in fantasizing about sex. As the use of pornography increases, so does the fantasizing about having sex with multiple women. The more the mind is fed with ideas about how to have sex in a variety of ways and with a variety of partners, the more the cravings increase. This is why it is called an addiction. To get the same level of satisfaction, the need for pornography increases.[15]

Masturbation takes it to the next level. With fantasies about sex with other women and images and video available to replicate what this could actually be like, a person's desire for more increases. This increase in desire, along with masturbation, causes physical and psychological changes within a person—changes that now makes him addicted to sex.[16] With all three present, along with an intense desire to have sex, the next step in this downward spiral is to act out. When a pastor or church leader acts out this sexual desire with someone who is not his spouse, he is abusing that person. He has abused the power of his position and broken sacred trust with his congregation, which will cause significant damage for all parties. If he acts out his desires with a minor, it is considered child sexual abuse and he will face criminal charges. If he engages with another adult, he has failed to keep fiduciary responsibility with his congregation and abuse has occurred. He is likely to face civil litigation.

Remember that spouses of sex addicts are victims of their partner's porn use. Messages and feelings that they are not adequate sexually tremendously damage self-esteem and self-worth. Even more devastating are the shame and embarrassment that come when their spouse's porn addiction is made public and the church and faith community have to respond. Often the pastor may be asked to leave or be dismissed from the church, which causes the spouse to have not only marital issues but also financial problems, an unknown future, and how to explain things to their children.

It's crucial for pastors and church leaders to receive appropriate treatment for pornography addiction. A few sessions with a therapist or a pastor's apology and remorse isn't enough. Relapse is always possible for any addict. If a council has required their pastor to undergo pornography treatment, individual therapy, psychological testing, and followed all professional recommendations when they became aware that he was addicted to porn and they choose to keep the pastor in his position, they can be assured they have done their best to address the issue should relapse occur. But also know that if relapse happens and the pastor acts out with another person, litigation by the abused is likely.

It's critical for pastors and church leaders to conduct themselves in appropriate and respectable ways. Demonstrating behavior unbecoming to their office and/or offensive and abusive does not fulfill what God requires for the office of church leader. Exercising and practicing appropriate boundaries and interactions with others help pastors and church leaders make churches safe places for everyone.

Chapter 5
Avoiding Lawsuits by Ensuring Ethics

"Settle matters quickly with your adversary who is taking you to court. Do it while you are still with him on the way."

Matthew 5:25

SEVEN DEADLY LAWSUITS FOR PASTORS

In the last twenty years, the landscape in regards to lawsuits against churches has changed. During the early nineties, there were seminars that trained attorneys on how best to sue pastors. Taylor writes:

> The beginning of the 1990s revealed a startling increase in the number and intensity of lawsuits against ministers and churches. Seminars where lawyers could learn to successfully sue clergy sprang up around the nation. These seminars have drawn hundreds, even thousands of attorneys.[17]

Then later:

> An attorney who attended another such seminar in San Francisco reported that as a religious believer, the atmosphere was "sort of creepy." While other seminars he had attended rightly taught that clergy who have acted illegally should be held responsible for their wrongdoing, that seminar emphasized the large settlements and verdicts available to lawyers who sued clergy and their denominations, conveying an image of blood being poured into shark-infested waters.[18]

Taylor talks about how pastors need to avoid the "seven deadly sins," which could lead to "seven deadly lawsuits." These seven deadly sins include fraud, defamation, child abuse, sexual misconduct, clergy malpractice, invasion of privacy, and undue influence.[19]

Fraud

Fraud is most easily defined as "deceitful acts for illegal gain."[20] Aspects of fraudulent acts can be seen in a variety of areas. Here are some fraudulent acts that may occur in the context of the church. When a pastor misrepresents information on an important matter, such as not telling a buyer about the church building's cracked foundation, a fraudulent act may have occurred. Since all critical and crucial information about a transaction needs to be provided at the time of sale, neglecting to be forthright with a buyer that a church rests on a landfill could lead to legal action later. Or if false financial statements are reported to church members and others, fraud may have occurred. This can be especially true in fundraising projects where others give based on the information provided.[21]

Maybe a simpler way to say this is if a pastor lies about what is going on in regards to selling something or he misrepresents something that leads others to believe what is not true, fraud may have occurred.

Defamation

Defamation is about damaging a person's reputation, character, or occupation through words or publication. *Slander* and *libel* typically describe this kind of behavior. However, in recent years, there has been less use of *slander* (defaming someone through spoken words) and *libel* (defaming someone through written words or pictures). A more recent trend is to put both acts into one word: *defamation*. Along with damaging someone's reputation and character, defamation can also be about exposing another to public ridicule and contempt or about broadcasting false statements about another.[22]

Certain criteria must be met in order to prove an act as the sin of defamation: actual use of defaming language, the actual statement targeted a certain person, the statement was in publication, and actual damage was done to the person's reputation. In the case of pastors, who are public figures, two additional elements must be included: establishing a pastor's reckless disregard for the truth and that the defamatory language was false.[23]

Pastors must be encouraged to use preventive measures to avoid defamation. By speaking well of others, showing themselves to be forthright and truthful in interactions and transactions, respecting the privacy of congregants and those of the faith community, and using care and good judgment when writing for publications, litigation because of defamation can be avoided.[24]

Child abuse

Child abuse is often viewed as one of the most serious acts of misconduct a church leader can commit. There are two kinds of child abuse violations involving pastors: (1) a pastor's sexual misconduct with a minor and (2) a pastor's failure to report known child abuse to authorities.[25] Criminal charges and civil suits can be filed against a pastor for these violations.

Most states require pastors to report child abuse or neglect to authorities within twenty-four hours of becoming aware of it. Reports can be made to the Child Protective Services of the county where the abuse happened or by calling the police. Investigation by the authorities will take place if the report fits the necessary criteria.

Failure to report can lead to some stringent consequences for the pastor, such as jail time and high fines. Litigation can also occur if it's discovered that the pastor knew about the abuse and failed to report it. In most states pastors are mandated reporters (with the exception of confidentiality in a confessional relationship).

To avoid criminal charges and litigation, pastors must know and follow the laws of their state regarding mandated reporting.

Sexual misconduct

Failure to establish and use good boundaries with others can lead to clergy sexual misconduct. Usually there are two kinds of boundary violations that relate to clergy sexual misconduct. One is when the pastor is a predator and preys on certain individuals to have his needs met. The other is when the pastor becomes carelessly involved with his parishioners. Whatever the case, pastors can know that it's likely they will face criminal and civil charges should the victim come forward with allegations of sexual misconduct.[26]

Civil liability, which means that the private rights of another have been violated, presents five arguments that must support the victim's charges of wrongdoing. These five areas include:

1. The pastor has more power in the relationship than the counselee.
2. The counselee typically makes herself vulnerable to the pastor, which may allow the pastor to take advantage of her.
3. The pastor holds a fiduciary responsibility to help others and not damage the counselee.
4. The pastor's proper representation of God has been violated.
5. The victim feels sexually exploited by the pastor.[27]

With this Taylor states:

> Any person who suffers injuries caused by sexual contact with a religious counselor, has a civil cause of action for recovery of all resulting damages.[28]

Criminal liability is also being adopted in some states. By breaking the law pastors who engage in sexual behavior with a counselee or parishioner can face fines, probation, mandatory counseling, and/or imprisonment.[29]

Clergy malpractice

Clergy malpractice is when clergy use negligent counseling practices and cause injury. Therapists, doctors, attorneys, and others must follow certain standards in their work as professionals. Because pastors are unlicensed and do not hold to a certain professional standard, it remains unclear what actions or behaviors are considered below a pastor's level of required care.[30]

When a pastor's care is considered below the required level of competence of other clergy and the counselee suffers injury, clergy malpractice is likely. When there are no set standards for pastors to follow, determining whether a pastor's actions are considered negligent or otherwise is something courts will need to decide.[31]

Here are a few challenges pastors face when the question of clergy malpractice surfaces. A pastor becomes aware that his counselee intends to commit suicide. Since there is no contract and typically no charge for his services, is the pastor required by law to report? If he reported, could it be considered a breach of confidentiality? Another challenge for a pastor might be discovering that his counselee has intent to harm or kill someone. Is a unlicensed pastor required to fulfill the duty to warn? Either choice could cause litigation for the pastor.

Invasion of privacy

Once trust has been built between a congregant and a pastor, the congregant comes to believe that he or she can share private information with the pastor and the pastor will hold that information in confidence. When trust has been established, the congregant will begin to seek out help from the pastor. A pastor's ability to develop trust with his congregants is key to effective ministry.

Taylor writes:

> If a minister is accused of invading someone's privacy, it is viewed by most as a serious breach of the minister's moral, and sometimes legal, obligation to that person. Such accusations shock our consciences, because we believe that protecting, not exploiting another's privacy, is the very job of those in ministry.[32]

Invasions of privacy can be viewed in four ways: "(1) intruding upon another's affairs or seclusion, (2) public disclosure of private facts, (3) false light publications, (4) and wrongful use of another's name or picture."[33]

Examples of possible acts that could constitute invasion of privacy are:

- A pastor appoints himself as investigator to determine if one of his congregants is having an affair.
- A pastor presents private facts and information about another publicly without the person's knowledge or consent.
- A pastor publicly presents false and skewed information about another, which causes damage to the congregant.
- A pastor uses someone's name or picture publicly without regard or respect for the person and without proper consent.[34]

To avoid litigation, a pastor must never involve himself in matters outside of his bounds and/or present information about another without proper permission. It's crucial for pastors to build and maintain trust with those in their care. Keeping information private and confidential is critical in doing that.

Undue influence

Undue influence is about exploiting a person by taking unfair and illegal advantage. Whereas fraud is about not being forthright about a transaction, undue influence is more about using the weaknesses or deficiencies of another for gain. In situations of undue influence, one of the parties is usually in a superior position over the other. For pastors, issues of undue influence arise when an elderly, ill, or impaired person agrees to give large sums of money to a pastor. It can be alleged that the pastor, who is superior in the relationship, somehow persuaded the individual to give the money, thereby taking advantage of someone who is weaker or more vulnerable than himself.[35]

How Does a Pastor Avoid Litigation?

1. Set and maintain healthy boundaries.
2. Consult with your council or supervisor before making any decision that involves privacy issues, money issues, or making public information about a congregant.
3. Always strive to establish and maintain a high standard of integrity and ethics for yourself.
4. Never overwork or underwork yourself.
5. Never make hasty decisions, which often lead to careless mistakes.
6. When asked to become involved in something of a personal nature with your congregants, be quick to say, "No thanks."
7. Commit yourself to a high standard of ministerial ethics.

Code of Ministerial Ethics Regarding Abuse in the Church

SOMETHING THAT MAY BE HELPFUL IN ASSURING A PASTOR'S COMMITMENT TO ETHICAL BEHAVIOR REGARDING HIS CALLING AS A CHURCH LEADER MAY BE TO PLEDGE TO KEEP A "CODE OF MINISTERIAL ETHICS." A CODE OF ETHICS FOR PASTORS CAN BE WRITTEN IN A VARIETY OF WAYS. THIS EXAMPLE IS WRITTEN AS A "PASTOR'S PLEDGE" TO CONDUCT HIMSELF IN SUCH A WAY TO ASSURE NONABUSIVE BEHAVIOR AND CONDUCT. EITHER AT HIS COMPLETION OF STUDIES OR AT ORDINATION, HE PLEDGES AND SIGNS THE FOLLOWING STATEMENT:

> Before God and these witnesses, I have responded to His calling to be servant to Christ and His church and promise to conduct myself in such a capacity that reflects Christlike behaviors.

In regards to sexual ethics, I, as pastor, promise:

To have sex only with my spouse.

To use appropriate interactions and communication with members and community via phone, e-mail, text messaging, and letters and end anything that becomes excessive, inappropriate, or harmful.

Never to be entertained by or engaged with pornography of any sort.

Never to touch another person sexually except my spouse.

Never to share personal or private information regarding my sex life with any congregants or church members.

Never to have same-sex partners.

Never to engage in long, intimate conversations about my personal affairs with congregants or others.

Never to have an emotional affair with anyone.

Never to speak about my sexual fantasies, dreams, and wishes to anyone or to share about past sexual encounters with anyone except my spouse.

Never to use any sort of sexual harassment toward any staff or church personnel.

Never to engage in texting or sending pictures of any pornographic materials to any member or nonmember.

Never to take sexually explicit pictures with my cell phone and send them to others.

Never to allow any inappropriate sexual materials in any of the church offices.

In regards to power and its potential abuse, I, as pastor, promise:

To use appropriate body language and verbal communication at all times in both public and private settings.

To use proper process and procedure whenever grievance issues occur.

To use e-mail communication appropriately.

To be truthful in all interactions with council, administration, and staff and be forthright in all matters related to the church.

Never to use threats, intimidation, anger, or physical harm to get others to comply with my demands or wishes.

Never to spread false allegations about another, whether verbal or written, including forbidding slander or libel of anyone.

Never to defame another.

Never to use alcohol to excess or get drunk.

Never to use illegal drugs or become addicted to prescribed medications.

Never to cuss or swear in front of staff or anyone else.

Never to divide a congregation into two parties or be party to causing divisions among church members.

Not to be participatory in poker, gambling, or other addictive gambling behaviors, including online gambling, slot machines, or visits to casinos.

Never to act on my own regarding decisions that must meet council approval first.

Never to become involved in another's financial issues or propositions.

Never to breach confidentiality of my counselees or members of the congregation unless legal involvement is necessary, such as duty to warn, and then only allowed by law.

Never to use stories or issues that have arisen from the members of the congregation for sermons, speeches, or presentations without written consent from the member to do so.

Never to show favoritism to some over others in my congregation or to be the cause of divisions among my staff or church members.

In regards to counseling ethics, I, as pastor, promise:

To meet with a counselee only when another is in the building and at least one other person knows about the session.

To remain seated in my chair behind or by my desk at all times; the counselee must remain seated throughout the duration of the visit as well.

To refer to a professional counselor when I feel the counselee's issues exceed my expertise.

To end the session immediately if I sense any flirtation occurring from either party and refer the congregant elsewhere.

To provide pastoral care and counseling only in my office, with the understanding that meeting in public places to discuss personal issues is prohibited.

Never to exceed a one-hour visit with my counselees.

Never to touch the counselee, including hugging and kissing, when alone in session.

Never to share personal sexual information with the counselee.

Never to do drop-in visits on congregants, with the understanding I must call ahead to make plans for a visit.

In regards to spiritual abuse, I, as pastor, promise:

To use Scripture appropriately in pastoral counseling settings, private conversations, and conversations with congregants and others.

Never to use Scripture or biblical references to threaten anyone, condemn them, or present God as an angry, vindictive God.

Never to use a rigid, legalistic approach to church leadership.

To welcome other perspectives, view, and opinions on issues.

With God's help, I promise to conduct myself worthy of fulfilling the high calling of pastor in the church of Jesus Christ.

Signature: _____ Date: _____

Witness:_____ Date: _____

Witness:_____ Date: _____

Witness:_____ Date: _____

Part 2
Responding to Abuse in the Church

Voice of Wesley Heersink

One of the saddest parts of my work as a victim advocate is to receive a phone call and hear the words, "I've been abused by the church, and I don't know what to do." These are the words I heard from Wesley Heersink.

Over thirty-five years earlier, a Cadet leader had sexually abused him and several others in the church. It was during camping trips that a man named Al did bad and shameful things to them.

After attending Cadets for some time, Wes remembers telling his mom that he didn't want to go to anymore. He never gave any specific reason why; he just didn't want to go.

A short time later, a parent from the church came forward and reported to the council that Al had sexually abused his or her son. It remains unknown who made the report, but Al was asked to resign from his position, which he did.

Wesley's memories of this time period are limited, although his brother, three years older than Wesley, recalls some of what happened. One instance occurred on a Wednesday evening after Cadets. The Cadet leader gave Wesley and his brother a ride home. As the three of them pulled up, Wesley's mom came out of the house to shake out some rugs. When Al saw this, he slowly let the car roll away from the yard light and then turned, kissed Wesley, and forced Wesley to touch him.

Nothing was ever said about the incident. It is now believed that Al abused many of the Cadet boys. Several of these now-grown men remember Al kissing, fondling, and sodomizing them during camping trips in the mountains.

Throughout his adult years, Wesley struggled with anxiety, depression, and health issues. He told me of being in and out of therapy, going to different therapists and group sessions, but he was never able to recover. He had severe diabetes and problems with light sensitivity. He often couldn't be in the sunlight without sunglasses or was unable to be outside before 3 p.m. He finally gave up full-time *employment because he was unable to meet the demands of his job. He then moved from California to Michigan to live in the basement of his mom and step-dad's home. During this time, he and his wife of three years divorced. She said she couldn't handle Wesley's issues, and he admitted that he was unable to connect emotionally with his wife.*

Then it happened.

In a group session, while thinking about his childhood and beginning to understand his depression and anxiety, Wes began to put the pieces together. He asked the leader if his experience of childhood sexual abuse could affect his ability to function as an adult. The answer was yes.

Once Wes was able to connect his childhood abuse with his adult mental health issues, he began his journey for answers. Several times, he contacted the church where the abuse happened and asked the leadership about any known history regarding the abuse of thirty-five years ago. He inquired about possible records and what could be done about the abuse now.

But the church was uncertain about how to respond to Wes. They had little to no records about what happened all those years ago. In one document, an elder and a pastor signed off on a conversation between the perpetrator and an elder, but exactly what had been said or done was not stated. It was understood that no punishment for the abuser occurred except that he resigned as Cadet Leader. There had been no call to the authorities, no involvement of child protection, and no interviews with other boys to see who else was victimized. There was no communication to the parents about what had occurred, and no direction was given to the parents about what to do for their sons. Wesley remembers that at a Sunday evening worship service, a council member went to the front of the church and announced that the boys were to, "Forgive and move on."

The church's initial responses were a disappointment for Wesley. It seemed that out of the Church's uncertainty about what to say, they responded with what first came to mind: "You wouldn't want to bring up all this now and hurt all of these people, would you? What good would it do…? Your diabetes isn't related to your abuse, and you could work if you wanted to.… We live in a broken world. You need to move on."

Wesley's frequent comeback for these arguments was, "You don't believe you have any responsibility or obligation to me? My life has been ruined and there is nothing left of it." He was looking for the church to take responsibility for what happened but wasn't finding it.

The council decided to take action in investigating what had happened. The Abuse Response Team of that classis met with both Wesley and the church's council to gather information from thirty-five years earlier. Following their investigation, the team sent a letter of recommendation to the church council. The council, however, neglected to follow the recommendations in the letter, and nothing was communicated to Wes about what they would do. Later they said they didn't know they were supposed to respond to Wes and tell him about what action they would take. Nothing had been done.

This was when Wes decided to appeal his case to Classis.

An appeal to classis meant that Wesley would come to the delegates of that classis and request a hearing about what happened to him and how the church had responded to his charges. His case would be presented to about sixty individuals, pastors, and church leaders, and they would be asked to review the church's decision. The delegates of the classis had the power to either sustain the church's decision or direct the church to do otherwise.

Prior to the actual hearing date, several issues surfaced. Wes requested that the hearing not be held in a church. With his PTSD and experience of sexual abuse, being in a church caused unnecessary stress and anxiety for Wes. It triggered too many memories of the abuse. But classis denied his request, and the hearing was scheduled to be held in a church sanctuary.

Initially the hearing was set to be an all-day event. There would be time to hear both sides of the issue, witnesses could be called, and there would be time for questions and discussion. However, the night before the hearing, the time was shortened to one and a half hours. This created added stress for Wes's team.

It's apparent that there was no way the delegates of this classis could have been prepared for what they were about to hear. With no information available to them until the evening before and with most of the delegates having little to no experience in responding to abuse, the delegates were challenged to understand the events that happened to Wesley (and others) and how properly to respond to his case.

The hearing itself demonstrated how difficult this was for both sides. The presiding officer failed to show impartiality; the pastor of the accused church blamed others for not knowing how to manage the process; many were stunned to see the skin breakouts on Wes's arms; and most of the delegates were brought to tears as they saw how hurt and sad Wes was because of the abuse.

What Wes wanted from the delegates was for them to direct the accused church to pay out to him a large sum of money and to give a moral apology. He believed that the church should admit that they had done him wrong, to admit that they failed to show responsibility when the initial abuse occurred and that they were now responsible for his disability related to the abuse. Because of all of this, he also wanted the church to pay out a large sum of money that would enable him to reach retirement.

Both were declined.

The delegates said that an apology a representative from the church gave to Wesley on the hearing floor was good enough. The Classis delegates didn't believe they had the power or the authority to require one of their churches to pay out large sums of money. The Classis offered to pay eight thousand dollars if Wes would close the case. Wesley refused.

Wesley was hurt. He appealed his case to the Synod of the denomination in 2006.

Again, Wesley wrote a letter about his case, and all the information from the initial hearing was submitted on Wesley's behalf. This time his case went to what is called the "Judicial Code Committee." After the Committee read and reviewed some of what Wesley's case was about, the Committee, led by an attorney, declined Wes's request to open and hear the case. In fact, the Committee said that it was not appropriate for their committee to make rulings on such cases.

So on the floor of Synod 2006, it was voted that Wes's case would not be opened or heard, therefore prohibiting any of it from being discussed on Synod floor. Wesley's case was closed and done with. No appeal process was allowed on the Synod level, although the Manual for Christian Reformed Church Government assures it.

Instead, the Judicial Code Committee, with the approval of Synod 2006, recommended and agreed that the Board of Trustees of the Christian Reformed Church would appoint a task force to design a mechanism to respond to abuse cases like Wesley's.

Just a few weeks after this, I received a phone call that Wesley Heersink had died. His mother had found him on her sofa after returning from the store. Nine-one-one had been called, but it was too late to resuscitate him. An autopsy showed that the arteries to his heart were blocked and a printout of his sugar levels showed they had spiked to five hundred in the months prior to his death. A small funeral with thirty-five attendees, including family and friends, was held. The basement he lived in for the last several years contained his belongings—all he owned after forty-nine years of life.

A few weeks after Wesley's death, I spoke with one of the pastors who had attended Synod 2006. When I shared with him that Wesley had died, he told me he had spoken with Wesley in the hallway during Synod's discussion of what to do with the case. Although he didn't know Wesley, he had asked

Wesley if he was a child of God. *The first two times Wesley wouldn't answer, but the third time Wes said he was.*

It took about three to four years for these events to unfold. After the hearing with Classis, Wes told his brother he was tired. He was tired of living and tired of fighting. He asked his brother never to resuscitate him. He wanted to go. Things were over for him.

For Wesley, approximate justice from the church never came. A written and public apology by our Synod 2006 would have proven healing. Money for bills and psychiatric treatment would have proven helpful. But nothing was done.

Sadder yet is the harm Wesley suffered in coming forward. The shame, the blame, and the refusal to do anything resulted in him being revictimized, retraumatized, and "reabused" by the church.

Working as an advocate for Wesley and for the Heersink family, I have found the church system's response a great disappointment. It seems that our pastors and church leaders lacked understanding about how devastating and horrific childhood sexual abuse can be. Pair that with the abuse occurring in the context of the church, and the damage becomes even more magnified. This is not to blame our church leaders, but rather to call for an awakening that we all need to work harder at understanding abuse and its effects. We must learn how to respond appropriately to an abuse victim, especially in the context of the church.

Hear the voice of Wesley Heersink. See his tears and know that his pain was real. His desire for peace never came. We had the opportunity to be Christ to our brother Wesley, but our hearts and our church system said no.

Hear the voice of Wesley Heersink, because the Christian Reformed Church didn't. The silencing of his cries, the minimizing of his broken heart, and the excuses that we can't do anything about this are shameful reminders of how poorly we were church and Christ to Wesley.

God heard the voice of Wesley Heersink and responded to his cry and intervened by giving what we chose not to: PEACE.

Chapter 6
Why We, the Church, Must Respond

Therefore, strengthen your feeble arms and weak knees.
Make level paths for your feet,
so that the lame may not be disabled,
but rather healed.

Hebrews 12:12–13

TYPES OF RESPONSES FROM THE CHURCH

There are many ways councils can respond to allegations of abuse. They could:

- Avoid the issue and not respond to it.
- Deny that such a thing could happen.
- Blame the victim.
- Partially address the allegations and then close the case.
- Dismiss the pastor without substantial evidence.
- Tell the victim to, "Forget it and move on."
- Make an agreement to silence the parties involved.

None of these are healthy or appropriate.

Why do we need to respond when abuse by a church leader has occurred?

Because it's the right thing to do.

Christ represents to us and to the world two things: *righteousness* and *justice*. Our broken world needs both because otherwise sin would reign on the earth and nothing would stop it. Destruction and evil would be everywhere, all of us doing as we saw fit in our own eyes. Life on earth would be impossible.

Striving to establish and maintain justice is crucial for the mission of the Christian church. Bringing justice to people who have been wronged, abused, or violated is necessary if we want brokenness to be healed, hearts to find peace, and the forgiveness process to begin.

When the church abuses, it has strayed from what Christ wants it to be—an agent of healing for God's broken world. If there's any safe place on the earth, it should be found within the church. However, in recent times, we are finding more and more that such things are not always true. The church has been an agent of harm and destruction for many.

Does it work to "Forget it and move on?"

No. And the church has told many a victim to do that. We should never deny or ignore such a horrendous evil and wrong. We should never send messages about forgetting it and moving on. We need to deal with the allegations as best we know how, hold wrongdoers accountable, and expect honesty and justice to prevail.

Abuse in the context of the church does immeasurable damage. It affects us emotionally, spiritually, physically, and sexually. It blocks and confuses our relationship with God, our worship of Him, and what the church is supposed to represent. The abusive church leader betrays trust, abuses power, and steals from those he was called to serve. God expects us to hold each other accountable for wrongful behavior no matter who we are: pew members, church leaders, or pastors.

Peace, peace when there is no peace

Jeremiah says:
> "From the least to the greatest, all are greedy for gain;
> prophets and priests alike, all practice deceit.
> They dress the wound of my people as though it were not serious.
> "Peace, Peace," they say, when there is no peace.
> Are they ashamed of their loathsome conduct?
> No, they have no shame at all; they do not even know how to blush." (6:13–15)

When there has been abuse by the church, it may fit better to paraphrase it this way:

> From every level of the church system, all want to gossip and shame for gain.
> Church leaders and pastors, council to administration, all practice slander and deceit.
> They look at your injury as no big deal.
> "Forget it and move on," they say, when in your heart of hearts, you can't.
> Are they ashamed about how they treated you? No, they haven't given it a second thought.
> They don't even know how to apologize and ask for your forgiveness.

When someone has been abused or falsely accused or victimized by the church, know that the pain runs deep. Sleepless nights, inability to concentrate, intrusive thoughts, painful memories, anger about the lying and deception, and the betrayal of trust cannot be easily erased. Anger at the church is appropriate and healthy. Refusal to accept simple solutions and pat answers from leadership is necessary. Know that when abuse by the church has occurred, *there is no peace.*

Peace comes only when justice has been sought and served. Know that the pain will lessen and the anger will soften once accountability and punishment has been administered to the abuser. Know that the victim will not and cannot trust the church fully again simply because the violation was that great. Know that the church must respond to abuse, fully and responsibly, so peace can come to all who have been hurt.

Why we must have a response plan

It's difficult for council members to be faced with the challenge of trying to sort through how to proceed when allegations of abuse come to their church. For those who have been through it, you know the amount of time and energy it takes to address anxious victims and their families, as well as how to help the secondary victims and others hurt by the abuse.

That is why having a clear plan in place about what your council will do if allegations come forward is very necessary and crucial. Some have said that they don't need to know anything beforehand. It's "no big deal," they say. Know that if you believe in the "I'll deal with it [the abuse allegations] when it comes to my desk and don't need to know or do anything ahead of time" approach, which I was clearly told by a pastor, you are running a high risk of responding in a reckless and careless way. This kind of attitude is likely to harm innocent parties and victims, and in the end, everyone will lose, including the church leader.

If church leaders have a plan in place, you will be more able think clearly about what to do and how to do it. In this kind of crisis, church leaders must strive to serve the victim, the victim's family, the congregants, and the offender and his family in a healthy, calm, and focused way. Having a spelled-out plan in hand can help with that.

The authors of *When a Congregation Is Betrayed* share helpful information about the importance of responding well to abuse allegations when they come forward:

> How would people respond if a deranged bomber were to succeed in blowing up a building filled with innocent adults and children? And, after a long period of confusion and dithering by officials, who knew the bomber well, a single ambulance appeared to whisk away only the bomber? And, meanwhile, all direct victims, the family members of victims, and those in the wider community who were thoroughly traumatized by the event were left to fend for themselves?[36]

Then:

> To summarize the old way of handling these cases, the offender was sent to treatment, given financial assistance, and often given a "geographical cure." The victim/survivor received at most a small financial settlement, often in return for silence. Because nothing was revealed about the abuse, all those secondarily affected were ignored. Even if a case became public, no thought was given to the needs of the congregation.

> In a more effective practice of triage, the old order is reversed, so that the needs of victims/survivors and all secondary victims take precedence over the needs of the offender. This new practice represents a radical change and can be expected to meet a lot of resistance. Of course, the offender does need assistance from the faith community, yet the others need more—much more. A just response for everyone must prevail if any religious tradition is to survive, even thrive, in good

health.[37]

The Church *Must* Respond to Abuse

There is no choice in the matter. We, the church, must respond and *respond well* when abuse allegations come forward. We must bring healing and justice to those who have been abused by church leaders. We must hold the wrongdoers accountable. We must reach out to help those who have been hurt and take a strong stand against any denial, avoidance, or minimizing of the abuse.

We, the church, must respond because it is the right thing to do. In the Psalms, we read, "Blessed are they who maintain justice, who constantly do what is right" (106:3) and "The Lord loves righteousness and justice; the earth is full of his unfailing love" (33:5). Amos says, "Hate evil, love good; maintain justice in the courts" (5:15).

To councils, I say, abuse is a hard subject to deal with, but you must. Let go of your cowardice, your passivity, and your insecurities. Let go of your need to have others' approval and acceptance, and take a stand against wrong and seek out what is right. Find wisdom and strength in God. Be strong in Him and seek Him with all your heart, especially when those times are difficult, especially when those times are about abuse.

Chapter 7
What Must Be Present in Responding

I looked for a man among them who would build up the wall and stand before
me in the gap on behalf of the land…but found none.

Ezekiel 22:30

In the last fifteen years, the Catholic Church has been bombarded with allegations of clergy sexual misconduct. Victims have shared that the abuse that happened to them in the Catholic Church has done great damage, and the Catholic Church's failure to respond properly only added to their shame and pain.

Before we shake our finger too harshly at the Catholic Church, let's acknowledge that abuse happens within the walls of all church denominations. We must examine what needs to happen during the response process and what makes an effective response process.

WHY VICTIMS OF CHURCH LEADERSHIP ABUSE DON'T COME FORWARD

- *No one will believe me.*
- *I will get blamed for what has happened.*
- *What will it do to my name?*
- *I might be revictimized and retraumatized by the church.*
- *Pastors protect abusive pastors within a classis.*
- *I'll lose friends and family.*
- *No one will do anything anyway.*
- *I'm expected to forgive and forget.*
- *Women exaggerate.*
- *I don't trust what the council may say or do.*
- *Slander and gossip are too prevalent in our churches.*
- *Church leaders tend to breach confidentiality.*

What Victims of Church Leadership Abuse Need When They Come Forward

- To be believed.
- To be told it's not their fault.
- To be listened to.
- To be given emotional support.
- To know that justice must prevail.
- A time and place to share their story.
- To receive pastoral care.
- To be treated with respect.
- Financial support.
- To be heard.

Acts of Justice

Justice must be present to bring healing and recovery to the victim. Marie Fortune, a leader in the field of understanding and responding to abuse in the context of the church, believes there are "Seven Elements of Justice-Making" that must be present when churches respond to abuse:

- *Truth-telling.* Break the silence surrounding the secret of the abuse. Give voice to what happened.
- *Acknowledge the Violation.* Hear the truth, name the abuse, and condemn it as wrong.
- *Compassion.* Suffer with the victim so that their suffering may be lessened.
- *Protect the Vulnerable.* Protect the victim from any more harm or potential abuse.
- *Accountability.* Confront the abuser, and expect repentance and consequences to occur.
- *Restitution.* Make symbolic restoration of what was lost; give a tangible means to acknowledge the wrongfulness of the abuse and the harm done and to bring about healing.
- *Vindication.* The victim is to be set free from the suffering the abuse caused.[38]

Truth-telling. Getting to the truth can be a difficult task. Cover-ups, lying, deception, not wanting to go there (either by the perpetrator or church leaders), fears of confronting wrongdoers, and fears of what the truth might really be are all reasons why churches are reluctant to move forward and find out the truth. Victims need the truth—they need it in order to heal. They need the truth so they can resolve things in their heart of hearts and begin to move on. Victims need to know that church leaders are aware of the full truth about what happened and aren't covering it up or silencing anything. Victims must know that the truth has been told.

Acknowledge the Violations. Call sin *sin*. If the allegations turn out to be true, then call it what it is: sin, wrong, evil. Church leaders can have a hard time with that. They are fearful of going that far—of calling sin sin. Although many of us were born and raised in the church, most of having gone through extensive catechism classes and Sunday training, faithfully attending Sunday worship, and familiar with what the Bible says, we may still lack the courage to call sin sin. Victims need to hear us call it what it is. We need to hear ourselves say it. When it's wrong, when it's evil, when it's against what God commands, we need to call it sin and condemn it as wrong.

Compassion. Jesus had compassion for the people. Matthew says if Jesus, "When he saw the crowds, he had compassion on them, because they were harassed and helpless, like sheep without a shepherd" (9:36). Then later, "He had compassion on them and healed their sick" (14:14). Mark 1:41 tells us, "Filled with compassion, Jesus reached out his hand and touched the man. 'I am willing,' he said. 'Be clean!'"

When abuse has happened, we must be people of compassion to the wounded. Compassion is about standing in their shoes and feeling their hurt and anger. Compassion is about weeping with those who weep and mourning with those who mourn. It's about identifying their pain and being able to express it in words and to say it back to them. And sometimes it's not about words; it's about being present with the person so they know they aren't alone in this trial.

When Jesus had compassion on the crowd, His heart went out to them. He saw their confusion, their lostness, their abandonment. And in that moment, He stopped and reflected and checked in on His own feelings and found His own sadness and hurt for them. That recognition of grief and sadness for another is called compassion.

This is what victims need. They need someone to stand with them in their pain and grief. They need fellow Christians not to be judgmental or harsh, not to try fixing things or dictating what they should or shouldn't do, but instead to stand in their shoes, hear their cries, and validate their grief and loss.

Protect the vulnerable. There have been times when I've told my clients, "I want you to wear a sign on your forehead that says, 'I am no longer available for abuse.'" That's what brothers and sisters in Christ need to do for victims of abuse within the church. We must wear a sign on our foreheads that says, "We will not stand for any more abuse in our church." Making sure no harm occurs to anyone else, we must do all we can to stop potential harm or abuse from occurring. By rallying around the abused, becoming a hedge of protection for them, and doing all we can to end the harassment, blame, and shame, we are protecting the vulnerable.

Accountability. It's important to hold abusers accountable for their behavior. Whether they have done illegal activity; used harassment, intimidation, or threats; falsely accused another; sexually abused another; or breached confidentiality—pastors, classis delegates, church leaders, and councils must hold wrongdoers accountable. That accountability must be thorough and complete and answerable for those who need to know.

Restitution. Nothing can undo what has been done. *Nothing.* Second best is all that's left. For recovery and healing, the victim must receive something tangible to symbolize that the issue has been investigated and dealt with, that a wrong was determined, and that "approximate justice" has been served. Money is usually the most common restitution for the harm done.

Vindication. The abuse will never be forgotten. It will always be a part of the victim's life. Because of this, the church must surround and embrace the victim with assurance that the church is sad about what has happened, will take responsibility for it, and will strive to do better in serving church members. The church must do its best to help the victim be set free from the hurt of the abuse.[39]

THE RESPONSE MUST BE SAFE

It's difficult for victims of abuse within the church to trust church leadership. Because the betrayal was great and because what they thought was a place of grace and mercy turned into being a place of harm, the abuse response process must be a safe one. Any sort of mistakes or errors, any sort of violation of due process, or any sort of confusion about how to bring justice to the victim increases the victim's burden instead of relieving it. Mistakes in process break the victim's trust again, causing revictimization and reabuse to occur. There must be no mistakes.

The question becomes: Can the church guarantee this? Can the abuse response process promise confidentiality, secure due process, and ensure objectivity? Can the abuse response system ensure no mistakes? Can the abuse response process demonstrate the competence needed so that victims are safe?

Medical doctors practice medicine. What this means is that they use medication to treat sick patients. They don't *become* medicine; they *practice* it. In the counseling field, a therapist practices proper ethics. Therapists do not become ethics; they practice it. So it needs to be with the abuse response system. They must practice "safety" and "due process" to bring to the victim and the accused a safe process that ensures, as best it can, objectivity and truth.

Someone recently said to me that it doesn't hurt if a few mistakes are made in the abuse response process. "People make mistakes; that's just the way it is. We just have to accept that." I say that the church has then abused her own people again. What was supposed to be gained in trust has just been lost. Again the church has failed.

There can never be a guarantee that the abuse response system is safe. It's something that is practiced.

ACTS OF REPENTANCE

In discussions about whether victims must forgive their abusers, Fortune presents this thought: Nowhere in the Bible is a case presented where a person who has lesser power and fewer resources must forgive someone with more power and greater resources. She explains that even as Jesus hung on the cross, wounded as He was, He did not say that He forgave those that sinned against Him. Instead, he asked the Father, who had more power, to please forgive.[40]

If, however, the victim believes that he or she needs to forgive, Fortune presents these "Acts of Repentance" to help the victim move toward the act of forgiveness. These acts of repentance are about relinquishing the abuser's power, which causes more equal power to be established between the victim and the abuser. Relinquishing the abuser's power can be done in these ways:

- *Restitution.* There must be restitution. Money for counseling or damages must be paid to the victim as a tangible expression that wrong has been done. This equalizes the power because the victim has received something back for wrong done.
- *Relinquish position and status.* The church leader must step down from his position of power. By reducing his status and power, he becomes more of an equal status with the victim, thereby allowing the victim to be more able to forgive. When a pastor has sexually abused a church member, the pastor is dismissed from his position. Or if a pastor has written abusive documentation about another and the allegations support that what he did was harmful and inappropriate, that role of administration ends and

he is banned from doing any similar work. Again, this is a step toward forgiveness by the victim.

- *Acknowledgment.* There must be acknowledgment of the abuse. By admitting he did it, demonstrated through verbal and written apology, power between abuser and victim becomes more equalized. By having the council acknowledge that, yes, the pastor did these things, the victim takes a greater step toward forgiveness.
- *Responsibility.* The abuser must take responsibility for what he did. By taking responsibility, the abuser demonstrates that he will do whatever he can to set things right, to show that he knows he did wrong and that he feels badly about it. It is hoped that the abuser shows heartfelt sorrow and remorse and that, by asking for the victim to please forgive him, he demonstrates that he is willing to take responsibility for what he did. This is another step toward forgiveness.[41]

To be more clear: The pastor/leader must say, "Yes, I did this. I am sorry. I was wrong and I hurt you. I take full responsibility for the harm I did to you. Please forgive me." His governing church body must do their part to offer payment for counseling services and damage that has been done. Also, the governing church body must take the steps of relinquishing the pastor's power by removing him from his current position. With this approach, power between the victim and the pastor becomes more equalized, making forgiveness for the victim more possible.

As church leaders, we are challenged to bring an effective response to our victims when allegations of abuse come forward. In a servantlike approach, we must strive to bring healing and recovery by using the "Acts of Justice" and "Acts of Repentance" in hopes of a better, more complete recovery process.

Chapter 8
How Does the Church Respond?

Rescue me, O Lord, from evil men; protect me from men of violence, who devise evil plans in their hearts and stir up war every day. They make their tongues as sharp as a serpent's; the poison of vipers is on their lips. Keep me, O Lord, from the hands of the wicked; protect me from men of violence who plan to trip my feet.

Psalm 140:1–4

Should a time arise when allegations of abuse by a church leader come forward in your church, know that it is likely to be one of the most difficult times your church and church leaders have ever faced. Amid the shock and pain of trying to comprehend that such a thing could happen, church leaders must respond respectfully and properly to all parties involved. I can't stress enough that the proper process of responding to allegations is crucial for the spiritual and emotional health of your congregation and faith community.

Should your work as leaders become sloppy, reckless, or fail to maintain proper process, litigation is likely to follow. Victims of abuse within the church come forward with the understanding that if the church doesn't properly respond to their cases, they will turn to the legal system for justice, restitution, and compensation.

It must also be noted that, for whatever reason, if a victim chooses *not* to take the church route or the legal route to address his or her allegations, he or she will use alternative methods of seeking justice, which can include submitting complaints to state licensing boards or reporting to other boards that govern nonprofit organizations.

A Word of Warning to Councils and Elder Boards

In the mental health field, there are diagnoses for personality disorders. People with personality disorders are difficult to work with. These individuals typically have problems within family and social networks. Skewed perception (what is really happening versus their perception of what is happening) is often a problem. Something that is black-and-white to most is a mass of confusion and distortion for those with a personality disorder. Lying is a typical problem that results from personality disorders. People with such disorders entitle themselves to read into things that are not there. Their skewed look at life can cause many problems when they need to have attention, want to have control and manipulate, or just prefer a chaotic way of life. Their history of conflicting relationships along with rejection and abandonment issues can cause some serious problems when issues arise in the church. Typically people with personality disorders are also victims of childhood sexual abuse.

Councils and elder boards need to be encouraged not to believe everything they hear, especially if it involves allegations about abuse by a church leader and the complainant is a victim of childhood sexual abuse. Too many times, I have heard that childhood sexual abuse victims have dealt with their past issues and are now cured. I am not convinced that is true. And I say this because victims of childhood sexual abuse repeatedly come back to therapy because their issues have been triggered. They aren't healed; they are *recovering* abuse victims. They relapse and old patterns of dysfunctional behavior return from time to time.

Two Church Polity Formats

What follows are ideas about how a Presbyterian form of church polity and a congregational form of church polity can respond when allegations of abuse come forward. This process won't work for all cases. The intention is to consider this a possible guide for councils/elder boards to use when addressing allegations.

For the purposes of this book, two terms are used to describe the governing body that leads the church and provides direction in addressing problems and issues. *Council* is used to name the governing body of a church that has the power over church employees such as pastor, ministry staff, and others. Typically, *council* is used in a Presbyterian style of church polity. *Elder board* is used for a congregational style of church polity. The power of a congregational style of church polity rests in the hands of the congregation. The congregation makes final decisions about discipline of employees. At times, both may be used simultaneously, but understand that both represent themselves as the governing body that leads the church and provides direction in what to do with problems and issues.

For this portion of the book, the word *complainant* will be used instead of *victim*. Likewise, *accused* will be used rather than *offender*. It's important to remember that a person isn't properly named victim until an actual abuse done against her is substantiated. *Complainant* also helps reduce prejudged thoughts and feelings related to the accused. Allegations are merely that—allegations. Only after determining the truth about an alleged abuse can the words *victim* and *offender* be deemed appropriate.

We know it's important to handle allegations of any sort with care and privacy, especially when in the context of the church. When a complainant comes forward to tell her story, it's crucial for her to present her charges in a way that gives permission for the council or elder board to move forward and address the allegations as well as keep her name and the allegations within respectful parameters. For the accused, he must be given appropriate opportunity to tell his side as well as be confronted when reports reflect concern.

The complainant discloses

The complainant or her support person must submit the charges in writing and present it to a council member (or an abuse response team member if the accused church has one). Without a written complaint or charge, the council will have a difficult time determining how to address the accusations. With written charges, communication about what has happened improves and rumors and gossip are reduced. When allegations are presented to the council in written form, the council can determine whether the charges are weighty enough to involve the work of a professional fact-finding panel or the abuse response team. Panels and teams have their own protocol regarding their work.[42]

In the Christian Reformed Church, guidelines for the function of an abuse response team are stated in the *Manual of Christian Reformed Church Government*, Appendix C.

Let's proceed assuming that the council has found the allegations weighty and an investigation is necessary.

Council assigns an advocate and a pastoral care person

The council will assign an advocate and pastoral care person for the complainant when the allegations come forward. An advocate is a trained individual with the important task of representing the complainant. The advocate's work includes helping the complainant understand her choices in the process; providing assistance and support through the process; helping with letter writing and attending meetings; speaking on the complainant's behalf; communicating with council representatives; helping with referrals to therapists, counselors, and legal counsel; and protecting the victim from revictimization and retraumatization.

The pastoral care person is a suitable pastor within the classis or region who is skilled in providing spiritual counsel and support during this process. To ensure objectivity, it is best if the assigned pastor is outside the council's church.

Step 1: Council begins fact-finding, investigative process

Council seeks out legal counsel

When allegations of sexual misconduct come forward, it might be wise to contact your church's insurance provider about what has happened. Your insurance provider will be able to give attorney referrals in your area should you need legal counsel. Typically, legal matters will stay out of ecclesiastical matters unless the victim files a civil suit.

Council requests a professional fact-finding panel or an abuse response team

If the council finds the allegations weighty and believes there is a need for more exploration into the allegations, they can request the assistance of a professional fact-finding panel or an abuse response team. Whichever is used, the panel or team will meet with the complainant to gather information about the allegations.

Panel or team meets with complainant

The purpose of the panel or team is to meet with the complainant and gather information about what has happened. The panel or team can also gather information from other parties who are knowledgeable about the alleged abuse. The panel or team reports back to the council.[43]

Therapy services and support group resources

The council offers therapy and support group services to the complainant and her family. The accused church should fund these services, or if the church is unable, the church's classis or region should offer assistance. If needed, therapists and support group leaders can provide reports of treatment progress to the council.

Panel or team reports back to accused council

After meeting with the complainant and compiling all necessary information into a letter, the panel or team reports their findings to the council. The report must state whether they believe the allegations are probable. If probable, the council continues the process. If not, the allegations are dropped and no further action occurs.[44]

Council informs the accused

If the council has decided to move forward with the allegations, the panel or team will ask to meet with the accused. The accused is informed in writing who the complainant is and what the allegations are, and a time and place to meet with the panel or team is decided. The pastor remains in his position and performs his duties while addressing the allegations.[45]

Therapy services and support group resources

The council encourages the accused and his family to participate in therapy and support group services. These services should be funded by the accused church (or the church's classis or region if the church is unable). Therapists can provide reports of treatment progress to the council, if needed, later.

Psychological testing, assessments, and evaluations

It may be helpful and at times necessary for the council to require psychological testing, assessments, and evaluations from the accused and sometimes from the complainant. Several tests can help identify areas of concern regarding the mental health of the accused and the complainant. Test results will give a narrative report about the profile of the individual, the type and level of dysfunction, and recommendations about what to do.

Step 2: Disclosure, education, and reaction

The council's initial disclosure meeting and letter

After a morning service, the council will disclose with discretion that allegations have come forward about the church leader and that an investigation/fact-finding process has been and is occurring.[46] This initial disclosure to the congregation does not require much detail or specifics, especially since the allegations are only allegations. Using wording such as "possible misconduct," "possible violation of boundaries," or "possible misuse of power" are safe and appropriate language to consider. *The complainant's name must be withheld.*

The next step following the disclosure is to send a follow-up letter to members of the congregation.[47] It might be wise to read or summarize the letter at the disclosure meeting to ensure that similar language is used in the meeting and in the letter. This may prevent congregants from reading into what was said: "This was said at the meeting but not in the letter."

Depending on the situation, after an initial disclosure occurs, the council may direct the pastor to take a "study leave." This temporary leave provides time and space for the pastor, congregation, and council to address concerns related to the allegations and how best to proceed.

Education reduces anxiety

Being *proactive* is always better than being *reactive*. It's better to have policies and procedures in place *before* abuse happens. However, things don't always work that way. Therefore when a church finds itself dealing with allegations of abuse, education about abuse will no doubt prove helpful. A better understanding about the topic of abuse, including abuse by a church leader, can reduce some of the anxiety about what has happened and answer questions church members may have.

Each church will have to determine the best time to provide education about abuse in the church. It could occur during or after the investigative/fact-finding process. Important topics of abuse education include: abuse of power in the church, how church leaders have fiduciary responsibility, appropriate boundaries, healthy relationships between congregants and church leaders, and the importance of holding wrongdoers accountable for misconduct. Education can take several forms, such as providing appropriate books and videos, hosting workshops and training about abuse, and inviting speakers to present on abuse.

Reaction to the disclosure

Congregants will need time and a place to process the disclosure. Providing opportunity for church members to meet one-on-one with church leaders may be helpful for processing. It seems that one-on-one meetings provide needed privacy and safety for members to share thoughts and feelings and can be a useful way to calm anxious congregants. These small meetings can be as simple as using a sign-up sheet approach with designated times and meeting rooms at the church.

Whether it's on the phone or in small meetings, council and church leaders must maintain confidentiality, discretion about what to say, and appropriate boundaries. There will be times when council members will have to respond with, "I cannot speak regarding that," "I need to end this phone conversation," or, "We can only wait and see what the panel or team reports." Being a good listener may be the best service at a time like this.

Step 3: Reports, action, and second disclosure

The council's report and action

The council collects all findings and reports and makes a decision about the allegations.[48] The professional fact-finding panel or the abuse response team's report, psychological reports, individual therapy reports, and even reports from advocates and pastoral care teams are to be reviewed and examined by the council of the accused. The council may consider consultation with involved mental health care providers, professional fact-finding panel or abuse response team chairperson, assessment providers, director of Abuse Prevention, or outside professionals and experts.

After careful review of reports and documentation, the council determines if the allegations and charges are true. If there is not enough evidence to substantiate the charges, the council drops all charges and the accused remains in his position. If the findings show that the allegations are true and/or other inappropriate conduct was disclosed during the investigative process, the council will determine disciplinary action appropriate for the offense. The council has the power to discipline and even remove the offender from office and/or employment.[49]

Second disclosure meeting and letter

Whatever the findings are, the council moves into a second disclosure meeting, and their decision regarding the allegations is announced. A second disclosure letter that uses the same language as the meeting is sent to all members of the congregation following the meeting.[50]

Reaction to the second disclosure meeting and letter

Since more information will be shared during the second disclosure than the first, it may be helpful to allow time for members to ask questions and express concerns at the second after-service disclosure meeting. When opening up the floor for discussion, remind the congregants that there will be some allotted time and, if needed, another meeting to discuss what has happened. Using small one-on-one meetings between council members/church leaders and church members can prove helpful.

Set and use appropriate boundaries at these meetings. Remember to set ground rules before the discussion begins, to limit the length of the meeting, and to redirect angry and disgruntled members. Encourage church leaders to model appropriate behavior and hold one another accountable during the meeting.

It's important for council members to find appropriate boundaries in disclosure meetings. Secrecy is not good, but neither is violating the accused by shaming or defaming his name. Consultation with your church's attorney prior to the second disclosure meeting may be wise.

Step 4: Recovery stage or appeal process

The council and congregation enter a time of recovery. See the next chapter for guidelines on how to properly bring recovery after there's been betrayal by a church leader.

The complainant or the accused can appeal the decision that was made. The appeal process is usually done with the next level of authority in the congregation's classis or region.

CONGREGATIONAL FORM OF CHURCH POLITY

In a congregational form of church polity, the power resides in the congregation. The elder board or its equivalent is functioned to help maintain direction and some decision-making for the congregation, but larger issues, such as the dismissal of a church leader, comes to the congregation.

Step 1: The complainant discloses and elder board responds

The complainant or her support person must submit the allegations in writing and present it to an elder board member. The elder board member presents the allegations to the executive committee of the elder board, and a determination of whether to disclose allegations to full board occurs.

Elder board discussions and appointment of task force

For this time, let's say that the executive committee of the board has decided to disclose the allegations to full board. The full board deliberates and decides to appoint a task force committee or hire a professional fact-finding panel that will be responsible to investigate/fact-find the allegations.

Elder board assigns advocate and pastoral care

The board will assign an advocate and pastoral care person for the complainant and her family.

Appointed task force or panel meets with complainant

The appointed task force or panel will meet with the complainant and gather information regarding the allegations. Upon completion of the interview and the gathering of information, the task force committee/panel will meet with the elder board to share findings and submit a report of such.[51]

Elder board reviews

The board reviews given materials from the task force/panel as well as other information that may have been relayed to them and they will determine whether to proceed with the investigation or terminate it. If not enough evidence has come forward, board may choose to close the case and all charges are dropped. If board finds the material weighty and probable, the task force is directed to meet with the accused.[52]

Therapy services and support group resources

The board offers to the complainant and her family therapy and support group services. Therapists can provide reports of treatment progress to the board if needed.

Appointed task force meets with accused

As directed by the board, the task force/panel contacts the accused, tells him about the allegations and who the complainant is, and requests a meeting with the accused. The task force/panel meets with the accused and gathers information and formulates a letter that contains what was disclosed.[53]

Psychological testing, assessments, and evaluations

It may be helpful and at times necessary for the board to require psychological testing, assessments, and evaluations from the accused and sometimes from the complainant. There are several tests that would help identify areas of concern regarding the mental health of the accused and the complainant. Test results will give a narrative report about the profile of the individual, the kind and level of dysfunction, and recommendations about what to do.

Elder board reviews

The task force meets with the elder board and shares a full report of their findings and recommendations about what to do.[54]

Along with that, the elder board collects and reads psychological reports and gathers information from other professionals involved in the case such as pastoral care persons, advocates, and therapists. The board determines severity and likelihood of the allegations. If it is determined that allegations are probable, board moves to first disclosure to congregation. If not weighty, all charges are dropped and the case is closed.

Step 2: Elder board discloses to congregation, provides education, and gives support after the first disclosure

After a morning service, the elder board will disclose, with discretion, that allegations have come forward about the church leader and that an investigation/fact-finding process has and is occurring. The complainant's name must be withheld.[55]

Then a follow-up letter must be sent out to members of the congregation following the disclosure. It may be wise to read or summarize the letter at the disclosure meeting to ensure that similar language is used in the meeting and in the letter.[56]

Education

Being proactive is always better than being reactive. It's always better to have policies and procedures in place before abuse happens. However, sometimes things don't work that way. Therefore when a church finds itself dealing with allegations of abuse, education about abuse may prove helpful. Having a better understanding about the topic of abuse including abuse by a church leader can reduce some of the anxiety about what has happened and answer some questions that church members may have.

Each church will have to determine when it's the best time to provide education about abuse in the church. Important topics of abuse education can include: abuse of power in the church, how church leaders have fiduciary responsibility, appropriate boundaries, healthy relationships between congregants and church leaders, and the importance of holding wrongdoers accountable for misconduct. Education can take several forms such as providing appropriate books and videos, hosting workshops and trainings about abuse, and inviting speakers to present on abuse.

Support

Congregants will need time and a place to process the disclosure. Providing opportunity for church members to meet one-on-one with the elder board may be helpful for processing. It seems that one-on-one meetings provide needed privacy and safety for members to share thoughts and feelings and can be a useful way to calm anxious congregants. These small meetings can be as simple as using a sign-up sheet approach with designated times and meeting rooms at the church. Being a good listener may be the best service at a time like this.

Step 3: Final congregational meeting to determine outcome

The elder board will call a final meeting to disclose information regarding the reports and findings and the congregation will be given opportunity to discuss and determine outcome of what to do with the church leader. If one meeting proves not to be enough or more time and research is needed, congregants can make a motion requesting so.

The congregation follows their church's protocol about discussion of the case. Discipline and dismissal of the church leader follows the church's policies.

Step 4: Recovery stage

The elder board and congregation enter a time of recovery. See the next chapter for guidelines on how to properly bring recovery after there's been betrayal by a church leader.

IF THE VICTIM CHOOSES LITIGATION

As victims come forward and tell their stories of abuse within the church, it seems that the option to choose civil action is becoming more and more possible. Since betrayal has occurred, it seems only logical for victims to choose the civil route. They fear that if they were to put themselves under the church's authority to investigate and handle the abuse allegations, victimization and abuse might happen again.

The church, it seems, quickly criticizes the victim when she chooses legal action. Apparently some read that resolving conflict by going to the judges, which the Bible speaks about, is parallel—that litigation and legal action are sin. In one case, the victim, after trying to be heard by the church about the abuse that had occurred, turned to civil action instead because the church had failed to respond appropriately. Her church leaders said that legal action was a sin and they threatened to put the victim under "church discipline."

The Church's Response

It remains the victim's choice of which direction she wants to do in addressing abuse by a church leader. If she chooses the civil route, the church must then decide what spiritual responsibility it has toward her, the offender(s), and their families.

Several aspects to consider:

1. Once litigation has occurred, attorneys will silence the church's desire to interfere. This means that any meetings the church may want to have with the victim or the offender will be discouraged and any persuasion the church may want to put on either party will be stopped. Once the lawsuit has been filed, attorneys do not want others to complicate the process that has begun.
2. If the church is insistent on knowing what is going on, they may opt to call the attorneys to see if any information or updates can be provided to them.
3. Most of us are unsure how the process of litigation works and what law terminology means. Once a victim begins talking with an attorney about her case, even before she has hired him or her, she can be assured that attorneys will explain how a lawsuit works, what some of the challenges may be, and will also help her understand the process. This may be a learning curve for the victim, the offender, and the church.

It's crucial for the church to ask itself what its responsibility is to the victim, offender, and their families when litigation is in process. The church can then best see itself to take a supportive role for all parties involved. This can include:

1. Assigning an advocate for the victim and offender.
2. Assigning a pastoral care team for the victim, offender, and their families.

3. For the council to engage in professional help in knowing what role would be best for them to take in addressing the spiritual needs of victim, offender, and their families as well as the congregation.
4. Offer financial support for therapy and counseling for both parties involved.

Once the lawsuit has either settled or has gone through court and trial, the church needs to reassess what needs to be done to help the victim, address steps of action against the offender if that is necessary, and bring healing back to the congregation.

1. If possible, obtain information about the lawsuit from the victim, the offender, and/or from court documents after the lawsuit has ended. Lawsuits are public information. Council members are encouraged to go to the courthouse and read court documents.
2. Determine from this information what steps need to be taken to address the behavior of the offender. Follow your church's discipline procedures.
3. Continue financial support for therapy and counseling for both parties for a limited time.

Steps for recovery from abuse in the church are addressed in the next chapter.

REFLECT AND REVIEW

Reading and thinking about what to do when your church is in crisis is often easier than actually carrying out the prepared plan. On paper we are mostly addressing the plan of action and how to do it. However, we know that when we put a plan into real life, the pain, betrayal, and hurt are greater than we could ever imagine. Abuse by a church leader can divide a church, anger the most saintly person, and turn a place of compassion and grace into a place of hatred and disharmony. We know that the unexpected happens during times like this and that Satan works hardest at our most vulnerable moments.

So many of you have walked this road, and so have I. We have seen and experienced the hurt and pain of betrayal firsthand and know we never want to go there again.

Remember: God's church must be a *safe church*. Let's strive to be a safe church in the best way church leaders are able.

Guidelines for Councils When Addressing Sexual Misconduct by a Church Leader
Diagram 8a: Presbyterian Style of Church Order

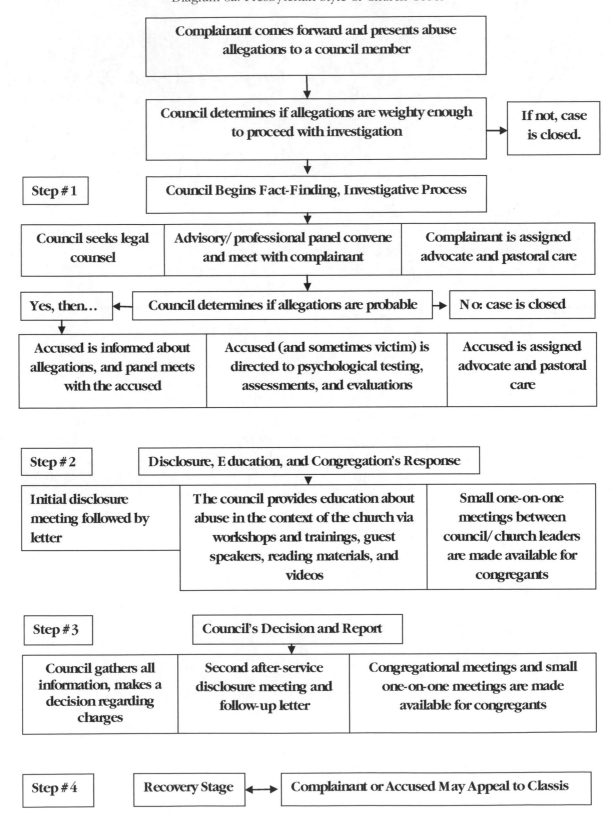

Created and compiled by Judy De Wit, MA, MA, LMFT See: *Manual of Christian Reformed Church Government*, appendix C

Guidelines for Elder Boards When Addressing Sexual Misconduct by a Church Leader
Diagram 8b – Congregational Style of Church Order

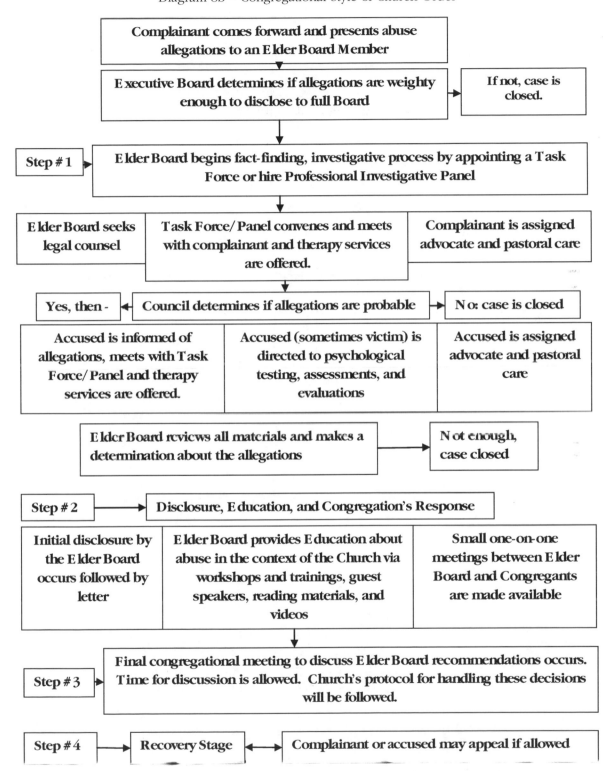

Created and compiled by Judy De Wit, MA, MA LMFT See: *Manual of Christian Reformed Church Government*, Appendix C

Part 3

Recovery from Abuse for the Church

Voice of Nehemiah

The burden of his heart was this: to rebuild the walls of Jerusalem, the city of his ancestors, the city of his people. With papers in hand, Nehemiah received permission to leave his home in Persia and travel to Jerusalem to rebuild the walls of that city.

And those walls were in ruins. Destroyed years earlier, the walls that had provided protection for the city were no more, and the temple was an easy target for enemy attacks. Determined and focused, Nehemiah and his men set out to rebuild the city walls.

But not without opposition.

Harassment, insults, ridicule, threats, and sabotage were among the efforts to stop this project. Sanballat and his men hated the sight of the city being reestablished, the walls being rebuilt, and with every possible plan tried to stop Nehemiah's efforts.

But their plans didn't work. They didn't work because Nehemiah's approach to rebuilding was about two things: prayer and action. With fervent prayers and with an organized plan, he and his men boldly and courageously built the city walls. With swords in their hands and others keeping watch around the clock, Nehemiah and his men did their work. And they finished the project in fifty-two days.

But the rebuilding wasn't only about walls. Nehemiah saw other things that needed attention and change. He helped establish a fair government for the people, addressed profiteering by the rich Jews, and met the spiritual needs of the people.

Just as physical rebuilding and reconstruction are never easy tasks, rebuilding and reconstructing the walls of a faith community when harm has been done after a church leader has abused is just as difficult. Trust, anger, accountability, and confusion become cracks and weaknesses in the church's wall, and Satan easily targets reparations efforts, making congregations vulnerable to spiritual warfare. God's Word in our hands and prayers in our hearts are essential to provide the strength needed to do

61

this work. Criticism and hatred, hurt and attacks, may come from every angle, but like Nehemiah, we must persevere.

Hear the voice of Nehemiah. Hear him say to us that under trials and destruction we take the Sword of the Spirit, which is the Word of God, and we become people of prayer—prayers for healing, recovery, strength, and forgiveness. We become people of action—action to recover and rebuild, action to reestablish and restore, and action to move forward with God's help.

Hear the voice of Nehemiah. When abuse has happened in our churches, we must do all we can to rebuild the walls of our faith community.

Chapter 9
Recovery for the Betrayed Congregation

A horrible and shocking thing
has happened in the land:
The prophets prophesy lies,
the priests rule by their own authority,
And my people love it this way.

Jeremiah 5:30–31

How Does a Betrayed Congregation Find Healing and Recovery?

When betrayal comes to your congregation, recovery is crucial. Never assume that church members will be able to recover on their own. Instead, acknowledge that a process will be needed to help church members to heal and recover in healthy and positive ways. What follows are ideas of what might be helpful for your congregation in recovery after clergy sexual misconduct. I also hope you will be challenged to think more deeply about underlying issues that might otherwise go unnoticed. This information can be modified and adjusted to fit other crises a church might find itself in. For now, let's assume that the accused church leader has been found guilty of sexual misconduct against another adult and has been dismissed from office. The church is without a lead pastor (see diagram 8a).

Church Council of the Accused

With CRC church polity, the power resides with the council of the church. When allegations of abuse come forward, the decision about what to do with the allegations and how to proceed rests with the council.

This is also true in the healing and recovery process in the aftermath of clergy misconduct. The council needs to determine who should help, how to help, who needs help, and some of the goals of the recovery process.

After the accused has been dismissed, the council is faced with a difficult question: "What now?" The congregation is reeling from the events that have occurred. They are feeling angry and confused over why a church leader would do such a thing, are in a state of shock and disbelief that it really happened, and are faced with the uncertainty of who can be trusted.

WHO HELPS?

With the council taking the lead, three additional parties can be included in the congregation's recovery process:

1. a council-appointed task force
2. an afterpastor or interim pastor
3. professionals and/or consultants

A council-appointed task force

It's typical for council members and church leaders to feel exhaustion and weariness at this stage of the process. They have spent weeks and months addressing the abuse allegations, and burnout is likely. To alleviate some of those pressures and to provide some new energy and perspective, Benyei et al. speak about the council's need to appoint a task force to help with the recovery process. These council-appointed task force members must consist of individuals who fully understand that the pastor's removal from office was an appropriate action while also being able to empathize with laity who is angered because of his dismissal. It is advised that volunteers not be used for this work because of possible underlying alliances they could have had with the dismissed church leader. Task force members *must* be appointed by the council.

Afterpastor or interim pastor

As Benyei, et al. writes:

> Afterpastors make reparations to the office of ministry by exercising emotional neutrality, establishing clear boundaries, and rebuilding trust in pastoral relationships. Afterpastors who conduct their business and interact with others in ways that consistently instill confidence, display predictability, connote truthfulness, and evidence authenticity will restore to the office respect and worth, and accord to themselves the support and resources needed to greater effectiveness.[57]

It's no easy job to be an afterpastor or interim pastor. Coming in on the aftermath of clergy misconduct is often stressful and sad, and great skill is needed to process and calm the hurt, anger, and confusion that seems to be everywhere. Several goals of afterpastors are to reinstate good practice of boundaries, demonstrate what healthy interactions in ministry look like, and strive to restore trust back to the pastoral office.

Interim pastors, who are typically used in the Christian Reformed Church denomination, must be individuals who have great patience and love for a people who are deeply hurt. They also will strive to bring healing, trust, and truth back to the office of pastor.

Professionals and/or consultants

All of the emotion that comes with recovering after a pastor has betrayed is great. Professionals and consultants can provide guidance and understanding about what the congregation feels and how to address those who are hurting. The professionals should be accessible for all three of the parties helping, including the council, the afterpastor/interim pastor, and the task force. Professionals and consultants, who are outside the church membership, provide an unbiased viewpoint and are experienced in how to help.

How to Help

With the four groups available to help in the healing process (council, task force, afterpastors/interim pastors, consultants/professionals), the question is, "How do we do this? How do we bring healing to a betrayed congregation?"

Education

Anxiety about something usually means that we are scared because we don't understand what it means. Education, including education about abuse in the context of the church, can help calm anxious hearts and minds. Questions that often surface are:

- Is this adultery or abuse?
- Why would this be called abuse?
- What if the victim is lying?
- What does abusing power mean?
- Can't we just ignore what happened?

In one instance, a victim could not understand the concept that the pastor holds the power in the relationships he has with his congregants. Finally, it was said to her, "What do you call him when you are in bed with him?" She responded, "Pastor John." Since her "lover" was still pastor to her, there was no equality in the relationship. He held a position of power over her and was abusing his power.

Benyei et al. speak about how pastors have fiduciary relationship and responsibility to their congregations. What does this mean? It means that because of the position the pastor has, he has the responsibility to hold the relationship with his congregants in sacred trust. When he breaks that trust by violating a member of the congregation, trust between him and the entire congregation has been broken. Therefore, because it is his fiduciary duty to maintain appropriate boundaries in relationships with his congregation, he, not the victim, is at fault for the wrong that has occurred. This also makes it abuse.

Healing service

Effective healing services can be done both publicly and privately for victims, their families and the congregation. The goal for a healing service is to bring an opportunity for the victim, her family, and the congregation to reflect and release the anger, hurt, and confusion for what has occurred. It would be hoped that the beginning of the forgiveness process would occur and the search for peace could begin.

One-on-one meetings

In the aftermath of clergy misconduct, there are many emotions and feelings that need to be processed. One-on-one meetings can provide an opportunity for that to occur. What is helpful about one-on-one meetings is that they are private so that individuals have the freedom to say what they need to say without others hearing their concerns. The council and/or the appointed task force can arrange these sign-up times at the church.

Small groups

Benyei et al. suggest that small groups of church members can be an effective way for members to process their thoughts and feelings. These small groups can be facilitated by council members or task force members and provide opportunities for members to learn from others about what happened. As groups meet and discuss, church members may begin to see a broader understanding of how prevalent abuse is in our culture and how we can respond better to it.

Spiritual reflection

For those of us who know what it feels like to be thrown into a time of shock and disbelief, it is no surprise that when the dismissal of a pastor occurs we ask, "Where is God?" Benyei et al. talks about the need for church members to do personal reflection on the events by searching the Scriptures for answers, challenging ourselves to look honestly at what caused this, and to try to understand what God is trying to say to us in the midst of it all. As ethical dilemmas surface and the realization that a congregation may have enabled such behavior to get that far, it's hoped that our relationship with God will be strengthened and an awareness of self increased.

WHO NEEDS HELP?

Victims and their families

Victims and their families are of primary concern for the council and congregation. Not only should the professional services be offered, implemented, and provided for the victim and her family, but also the church leaders and congregants must show support, love, and concern for the victim. She needs to feel embraced and welcomed into fellowship with no grudge being held against her. It's helpful for the victim to know that the church has called this "wrong and sin and disgusting" and their anger is directed to the person who did it. It's important for the Church to remember not to blame the victim for what has happened.

Council and lay leaders

Typically much time and energy are invested between the leadership and the pastor of a given church. Many council members assume that the pastor can be trusted and that they will do their job respectfully and appropriately. However, when a pastor is found guilty of sexual misconduct, council members feel their own betrayal and confusion. Suddenly time and energy are pulled away from ministry tasks and addressing pastor misconduct becomes precedent. This kind of church work takes its toll and the exhaustion in dealing with the allegations and charges emotionally drains church leaders. They as well as anyone else need the support and encouragement from each other, professionals, and area pastors.

Volunteer and paid staff

Acts of manipulation of staff are typical behaviors of an abusive pastor. (Benyei et al. 2006) His ability to create jealousy and divisions among his staff by making certain individuals feel special and indispensable and others unimportant and insignificant will cause the existence of two camps on a church staff. The loyal ones will remain faithful to him no matter what happens while the disregarded ones will be angered by unfair treatment. Therefore, once the pastor has been removed from office, providing outside-of -the—congregation consultants to meet with the staff will prove necessary and critical. Building up and restoring unity among church staff is important in the healing process.

Professional staff/clergy

Professional staff and clergy are often those who know the abuser best. Their history with the offender can go back to seminary days, shared committee work time, or the confiding with one another about laity problems. With energy and trust invested in the offender, it's painful for professional staff and clergy to believe and accept that the one they knew well had participated in behavior that is so contrary to this sacred office. Benyei et al. stress the need for support and counsel as they bear the large burden of losses, both for the congregation and for themselves.

Congregation

For those of us who have witnessed the response of a congregation after disclosure of clergy misconduct or who ourselves have known betrayal, differing views, opinions, and camps are inevitable. Providing opportunity and place for processing thoughts, feelings, and experiences are crucial in the recovery for the congregation. Whether done in small groups, individually, or with professionals, time to process, accept, and move forward will be needed.

RECOVERY PROCESS

Processing of emotions

If you have ever been a witness or been involved in a church where betrayal by a church leader has occurred, you know all about the emotional climate of a betrayed congregation. Anger, shock, denial, hurt, confusion, disbelief, anxiousness, fear, paranoia, sadness, depression, despair, and rage are to name a few. It's not that any of these emotions are wrong or are inappropriate. Instead these emotions are quite accurate and are similar to grief and loss issues.

So the question that needs to be asked when dealing with a faith community that has been betrayed is this: How does the leadership of a betrayed church help their church members process their emotions appropriately and effectively so they can heal?

Grief Wheel

One place to begin with the healing process is to provide a time and a place for them for express their feelings about what has happened. Again, this can occur in small groups with church leaders or meeting individually with council members. Benyei et al. speak of emotions for a betrayed congregation as similar to what Chilton Knudsen uses in his grief wheel. The typical emotions that need to be processed by congregants are: denial, shock, bargaining, depression, anger I and II, and acceptance. Know that these emotions can go back and forth until finally acceptance is reached. Note that the difference between anger I and anger II is that anger I is the blaming of anyone for what has happened and anger II, which comes later, poses the question about how such a thing can be prevented from happening again.

Gaining trust and respect back for the office of pastor

Afterpastors and interim pastors have the difficult task of trying to gain trust back for the office and position of pastor. (Benyei et al. 2006) Often, because of the careless and reckless work of the offender, great efforts on the part of the afterpastor/interim pastor will be needed to show that he has consistency in his word and deed. This means that when the afterpastor says he'll do something, he'll do it. Because of past experiences with the previous pastor, the congregants' expectancy would be that he won't really do as he says, that he doesn't really mean what he says, and that disclosing anything with him runs a heavy possibility of violation. That is what the afterpastor must prove: He will carry through on what he says. That's foundation for getting trust back for that office.

As Benyei et al. writes:

> Afterpastors can heal the office of ministry by providing consistently solid basic ministry, by undertaking the ministry to which they have been called with respect and dedication, grace and humility, and by serving others without need to be revered or loved. Afterpastors do well to remember that competent ministry is intended to serve others, not to impress them.[58]

Reestablishing appropriate boundaries in pastoral relationships

Boundaries can be explained as simply as where a pastor needs to say no in his relationship with his congregants. Setting limits are crucial and necessary to establish and maintain healthy and appropriate relationships with others and also creates respect for both parties. Examples of appropriate boundaries for pastors are pastoral care visits should never exceed an hour, calling ahead to do a home visit is appropriate and respectful, and one should never counsel without someone else in the building. Boundaries are also about limits on what a pastor shares about his personal life, the appropriateness of hugging another, and prohibiting excessive and non-church related text- messaging and emailing to female members.

An abusive pastor typically has problems with setting and using appropriate boundaries. Congregants become desensitized to the pastor's poor boundaries and what is appropriate and inappropriate about a pastor's behavior becomes blurred. A congregation's defense to a pastor's poor boundaries can be that "he's just that way."

That's what makes the reestablishing of good boundaries so difficult in the aftermath of clergy misconduct. Sloppy and reckless behavior has occurred for such a long time that it seems normal. It takes much energy on the part of everyone to get healthy boundaries back to where they should be. Recovery to healthy and appropriate boundaries is a long and hard road.

Expectations for pastors

The council holds responsibility to hold pastors accountable for what they do. This means that when they are informed about boundary violations, about reckless behavior, about senseless comments and interactions, the council must take it upon themselves to confront and discipline as necessary. This is not to be a rigid, controlling approach by the council, but one that shows that the pastor is answerable to the council and the council will take responsibility to confront and deal with issues.

A spell out of what the council expects from the pastor must be made at the onset of his hiring. This and ongoing communication of what is expected from the pastor and his work in his position will ensure better performance and effectiveness in his service to the congregation.

Identify and eliminate controlling and manipulative approaches of pastors

It's important to know what controlling pastors (and church leadership) looks like.

Typically controlling pastors will:

- blame—it's always someone else's fault
- shame—others are viewed as lesser, their opinions don't count, they don't know things
- guilt—you should have, could have, why didn't you statements
- possessive/jealous—if they aren't the center of attention
- anger—their tempers flare easily when it doesn't go their way
- tell others how to think and feel
- disregard boundaries of others

Manipulative pastors tend to:
- work behind the scenes to get others to change their minds
- side with and validate those who have power in the church
- fail to practice good boundaries
- withhold information for personal gain
- fail to be forthright
- lie

IDENTIFY AND STOP: ABUSE, ABUSE OF POWER, DECEPTION, ENABLING

When abuse allegations are brought forward and charges are substantiated after the investigation, and the dismissal of the pastor occurs, it's time to look carefully at the function of the church leadership.

It's easy to blame the pastor for his behavior and he should be. But before we point the finger too much at one person, it is crucial to remember and know that the council and even church members must also take some of the blame. Usually in these settings, the council and church members have been inattentive to inappropriate boundaries and behavior. This inattentiveness can include not listening to complaints that may have come forward, ignoring their awareness that things don't seem right, and succumbing to their own need to be liked by the pastor.

Education and training on effective church leadership is an ongoing necessity. It's never safe to assume that church leadership knows how best to lead. Council members change yearly. And just because training occurred two years ago for them, doesn't mean that the benefits of that training are still happening.

Good leadership is practiced. It's not something that is automatically reached. Accountability, communication, checks and balances, and evaluation on performance are all ways to ensure better, healthier pastors and churches.

Moving toward transformation

It's fair to ask, "And where are we going with all of this?" The answer is: to enter the process of forgiveness, to do reconciliation work, to be a safe church, and to rebuild community and fellowship.

The forgiveness process

I've heard many discussions about this: How does one forgive when such a horrendous evil has been done by a church leader and within the fellowship of believers?

There is much to be said about how to forgive a church leader who has abused. It is important to remember that forgiveness is possible because we have God. To do this work we must be willing to put forth a conscious effort to do an act of forgiveness. It's always easier to harbor anger and build resentment for what has happened. It's always easier to let our anger turn into bitterness. Retaliation and vindictiveness are two easy ways. Forgiving and letting go are not. Forgiving is hard work. Forgiveness is never a simple, one-step process.

Forgiving is the right thing to do. It is what God requires. It is what brings healing to a person's life. Its life-long process of giving over our hurt to God and asking Him to help us do the difficult task of forgiving is God's greatest desire for us.

The transformation journey

It could be that the victim may request reconciliation between her and the offender or herself and her church. With a professional mediator, this should remain an option for the victim. Understanding and using conflict transformation may be helpful for victims. More of this will be shared later.

How to be a safe church

Policies and procedures for safety for all church attendees are an absolute must. Protecting our children in nurseries, our school age kids in our church education programs, and our youth in their activities, are all necessary to ensure that church is a safe place.

Adults must be wise in their interactions with one another and their church leaders. Guidelines help ensure healthy relationships including addressing issues of: one-on-one meetings, hugging, text messaging, e-mailing, and so much more.

REBUILDING COMMUNITY AND FELLOWSHIP

Rebuilding a faith community after the dismissal of clergy misconduct is more than a disruption or an inconvenience. It's like a train wreck, a tsunami, or a hurricane.

Thankfully, our God is a God of train wrecks, tsunamis, and hurricanes. And there is nothing He can't repair and restore if we ask Him to help us in the task. It doesn't mean that when He helps us that things will return to the way they were before. But it does mean that a disaster can bring about a maturity, a greater wisdom, and a greater knowledge of Him that was not there previously.

When people ask me about how long do I think it really takes to restore a church in the aftermath of clergy misconduct, I've learned to respond with, "A generation must pass on." This typically means about twenty-five years. Recovery is a long-term and ongoing process.

How to Bring Healing to a Betrayed Congregation
Diagram 9a

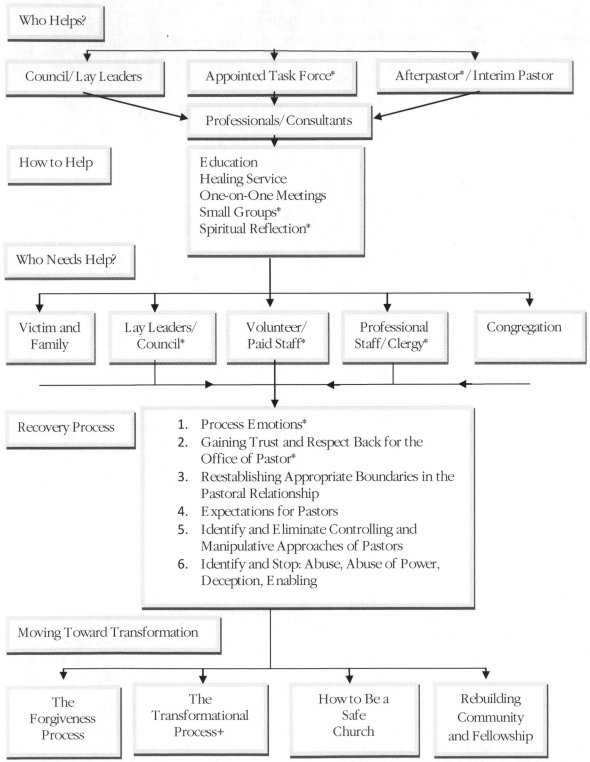

Who Helps?

Council/Lay Leaders   Appointed Task Force*   Afterpastor*/Interim Pastor

Professionals/Consultants

How to Help

Education
Healing Service
One-on-One Meetings
Small Groups*
Spiritual Reflection*

Who Needs Help?

Victim and Family   Lay Leaders/ Council*   Volunteer/ Paid Staff*   Professional Staff/Clergy*   Congregation

Recovery Process

1. Process Emotions*
2. Gaining Trust and Respect Back for the Office of Pastor*
3. Reestablishing Appropriate Boundaries in the Pastoral Relationship
4. Expectations for Pastors
5. Identify and Eliminate Controlling and Manipulative Approaches of Pastors
6. Identify and Stop: Abuse, Abuse of Power, Deception, Enabling

Moving Toward Transformation

The Forgiveness Process   The Transformational Process+   How to Be a Safe Church   Rebuilding Community and Fellowship

+John Paul Lederach, *The Journey Toward Reconciliation* (Scottsdale, PA: Herald Press, 1999). *Candace R. Benyei et al., *When a Congregation Is Betrayed: Responding to Clergy Misconduct* (Herndon, VA: The Alban Institute, 2006). Compiled and created by Judy De Wit, MA, MA, LMFT

Part 4
Transformed Because Abuse
Happened within the Church

Voice of Jacob

Twenty years have passed since Jacob deceived his brother, Esau, so that Jacob could claim the birthright. Jacob didn't leave on good terms with Esau. The last he knew, his brother was angry enough to kill him.

Now the two brothers are about to meet again. Jacob sent gifts ahead to Esau as a greeting, an attempt to appease his brother and ease some of the bitterness that might still remain. The evening before, Jacob made arrangement to have his family cross the Jabbok so that he would have some needed time alone to think and pray about the day ahead.

Many things came to mind as he thought back on the days when he and his mother deceived his father, how he managed to get away and flee to Uncle Laban's, and how angry his brother was. Jacob grieved as he thought about these events again.

Did Jacob regret for what he had done to Esau? Maybe. Did he see that he had wrongfully acquired a family blessing that every eldest was entitled to? Yes, he sees that. Does he see that his actions have caused issues of betrayal, breaking of trust, and a mishandling of respect for family and authority? Yes, he knows this. And now he must meet with Esau face-to-face and come to terms with what he did.

Jacob needs to make amends with two different people. The first is a man he does not know, a stranger. Jacob wrestles with until daybreak. When neither is able to overpower the other, the stranger is ready to leave. But Jacob is not ready to let him go. Years of conflict and hardship, years of strife and family problems, have taught him something: Resolving conflict is necessary and worth the effort.

This conflict is with God. For the last twenty years, Jacob has been running—from family, from problems, from God. Although life has been difficult, Jacob has grown in one important area: self-awareness. He clearly sees the deception, sin, and mistakes he has made in his life. He has come to terms with the harm he has done to family and others. He realizes that his brother has been deeply hurt by his deception and the stealing of the birthright. This self-awareness has enabled him stop and look deeply into his heart of hearts to see what he has done wrong. He finds remorse, sorrow, and regret.

As Jacob comes to terms of what he has done, he also knows that his God is a God of mercy and love and forgiveness. And so with that he refuses to let go of God without a blessing. That's what happens at daybreak. And God grants Jacob the blessing with a reminder: a hip problem.

One conflict resolved. Another is on the horizon.

As Jacob sees his brother, it's apparent that Esau has also changed. He greets his brother with a kiss, expresses happiness for seeing him, and wants to be with his brother again. As Esau discusses with Jacob the possibility of traveling and being together, Jacob is concerned about trusting Esau. Using the excuse that he has many young children, Jacob convinces Esau it's best to part ways.

Hear the voice of Jacob. He was abusive when he took advantage of his brother and then later experienced abuse when his uncle took advantage of him. He needed time to reflect, process, and mature in both situations. Having betrayed his brother's trust by stealing the birthright and having been betrayed by his Uncle Laban, he knew about two things: repenting and confronting.

Hear the voice of Jacob. Struggle, wrestle, and agonize. Then determine whether you need to repent of your sins and ask the victim for forgiveness or if you need to prepare yourself to confront the abuser, giving blessing to the one who has wronged you.

Chapter 10
Why Victims Want to Meet

For your face is like seeing the face of God,
now that you have received me favorably.

Genesis 33:10

In most cases, victims who have come forward to present allegations of abuse via either the ecclesiastical or legal route need to talk when the case has been decided upon and closed. In a few cases, victims have asked to meet with the perpetrator to resolve or reconcile. It's more likely that the victim will request to meet with the council of the accused.

By allowing victims to talk to the council of the accused, healing and restoration begins. By using their voices and being heard by the council of the accused, victims feel empowered and some of the healing process is underway.

ECCLESIASTICAL ROUTE

In most of the situations I am familiar with, the ecclesiastical route has not been a positive or helpful experience for victims. More often than not, when victims have come forward and presented their allegations, councils have not responded in constructive ways. The council's lack of understanding about how best to respond to victims frequently results in council members saying and doing things that increase rather than relieve the burden for the victim and his or her family.

Not only have councils been hurtful, but sometimes the work of abuse response teams also hasn't met the victim's expectations. Inadequate responses from council and failed work of abuse response teams increases victims' anxiety as they struggle with how to move forward and who to trust.

When the investigation is complete, victims typically want to meet and speak with council of the accused to share how their lives have been changed because of the abuse. Victims seek out the opportunity to share their pain and hurt in hopes of receiving a heartfelt acknowledgment from the council that their pain is real and is understood. It is healing for victims to have voice in what has happened.

LEGAL ROUTE

When churches do not demonstrate integrity and responsibility in responding to abuse allegations, victims may turn to legal counsel. If the church doesn't seem to want to give justice, victims frequently turn to legal system to get it.

There are pros and cons to going the legal route. One positive about the legal system is that attorneys will protect the victim and take the lead on what is best for the victim. When you have hired an attorney, you can be certain that the victim's voice will be heard. Attorneys make phone calls, access paperwork, and speak on behalf of the victim. Attorneys are hired to win and they will do all they can to make sure a victim has a voice in what happened and receives compensation for the wrong that was done. (Please be aware: If a case is settled outside of court, a gag order will be put on the settlement agreement. Victims must be aware of how a gag order affects their future. Whether to settle out of court or go to trial is the victim's decision.)

There are also several cons to using the legal system. When lawsuits are filed, records become public. This means that your case may be reported in a local newspaper, that others can have access to the documentation if they request it, and that any counseling records or similar material can become public knowledge. A victim must be prepared for this kind of public awareness and potential media involvement. Attorneys can also be expensive unless one is dealing with the defendant's liability insurance. In those cases, attorneys usually will take a certain percentage of the settlement money.

When civil litigation is involved, attorneys will typically involve only the church leaders who can provide information to strengthen the victim's case. The attorney may restrict the victim and his or her family from speaking to church leaders during the lawsuit. If this happens, the distancing between the victim and the church leaders will increase, which may become problematic since the church is unable to provide pastoral care and support to the victim.

If a victim has chosen the legal route over taking their allegations to the church, council members should be encouraged to go to the courthouse and read for themselves what happened in the case. It is the council members' responsibility to know what happened. Reading the lawsuit for themselves is one way to gain understanding about what the church leader did so that they will know better how to address the abuser and help the victim.

It is very encouraging for victims when council members care enough to go to the courthouse and read the documentation about a case. In addition, because the council members are properly informed about the details of the case, they are better equipped in taking the next step to address their pastor.

The church must never "terminate"

In a case I am familiar with, a victim litigated the church leader who had abused. Once the litigation ended, the church officials "terminated" the victim. This meant that the victim was no longer allowed to communicate with the church officials about the case although no other services were provided by the church system.

Termination is a clinical word, not a ministry word.

Church leadership is never to terminate anyone. When a case is closed or is resolved, the *work is just beginning.* So much must be done to find healing for the victim and the abuser and for the families and church members affected. Churches are not under contract for their services. Church leadership, including councils, classis leadership, and denominational personnel, are in no position to end services with the parties involved because the case is closed. In fact, their work has just begun in earnest. Finding healing and restoration in the midst of so much damage is a crucial task for the church.

Why victims want to meet

My experience has been that after the investigation is complete and the case is resolved, most victims want to meet with council of the accused. A victim's meeting with the council of the accused (often including accompaniment and representation by a well-trained mediator) can provide the time and place for the victim to use her voice and share what the abuse experience has included. Often, pieces of information may have been overlooked by or unknown to the council. This meeting provides an opportunity to bring the facts to the table and share the emotions that accompany them. The difficulty is that if a gag order is involved (if the victim has sought legal assistance and settled out of court), what is said and discussed may be somewhat restricted. An attorney can give direction about that.

Recovery from abuse by a church leader is a complicated and long process. It is healing for victims to have the opportunity to use their voice and be heard by the council of the accused. By being able to tell their story, the victim can begin to understand their own pain, and the power of the hurt and confusion lessens. As the council of the accused listens to what one of their members went through, the victim will hopefully feel their compassion. If the council of the accused truly stands in the shoes of the victim, healing will be the ultimate outcome.

Chapter 11
The Transformational Journey

But now in Christ Jesus you who once were far away have been brought near
through the blood of Christ. For he himself is our peace, who has made the
two one and has destroyed the barrier, the dividing wall of hostility.

Ephesians 2:13–14

In a city not far from where I live, teen suicide attempts—and successes—were becoming
rampant. It was a problem with no simple answer. Finally, when it got to the point that one of the
school superintendents also attempted to end his life, the community realized it had to come to
terms with what was happening. They began a desperate search for solutions, for steps to take.

After a series of interventions, business owners and community leaders came forward with
the realization of what (or who) they needed: God. And God is who they pursued.

Business leaders in the community began by having monthly prayer meetings to pray for
their community. As more and more of the community leaders heard about these meetings
and began to see their need for God, they began to realize that turning to God—and having a
relationship with Him—was the answer to their problem. As time passed, the monthly prayer
meetings continued to grow—until a total of five hundred people were coming to read Scripture,
pray, and eat lunch together.

The city was transformed.

Drug dealers left town. Suicide attempts went down. Billboards and signs with Scripture
passages went up. You cannot pass the Ford dealer's sign without seeing its Scripture passage for
the day. And one of the city's banks has become known as "The Bank Who Prays for You."

Now that's a transformation!

That's what can happen when conflict and problems come into our lives. What was bad and
ugly can, with God's Spirit, be changed into something meaningful and earthshaking. What was
harmful and horrendous can be changed into something spiritually deep.

The same is true for abuse that has happened within the church.

The transformational journey for victims, perpetrators, councils, congregations, and faith
communities can and should be a search for a better understanding of God. The journey through

78

these troubled waters should not cause us to drown or be diminished but should instead be an experience that brings us to a greater learning curve of who our God is and what He wants His church to be.

WHAT THE JOURNEY IS ABOUT

If you've been abused by a church leader, you will be faced with challenging and heartbreaking questions. Intrusive thoughts, restless nights, and anxious days will plague you as you try to sort through how and why this could have happened. At one point, you might think you are done with the process...and then the next day you will find yourself wrestling with it again.

Why does this happen? Because when you encounter abuse by a church leader, you are challenged with a God-purposed transformation.

Because abuse by a church leader is a big deal, the road to recovery will be difficult. Your journey to seek truth, justice, grace, and peace will be painful. At times, you will want God to just go ahead and punish the abuser for doing such a thing. And then at other times, your heart will soften and you will realize anew how frail and sinful humans are (including yourself). At times, your anger will get the best of you, and you will be harsh and critical about the church. Then at other times you will realize that the church is made up of sinners just like you.

Finding a balance between justice and grace is difficult. Victims and their families will want justice for the wrongdoing they have endured. Justice is needed. They will recall Bible stories about God's justice, and they will want punishment to come to the abuser. Others will recognize the need for justice but will also understand that God's grace is here for us as well. Determining how grace, accountability, punishment, consequences, justice, and mercy all come together is challenging.

GOD'S JUSTICE

When a church leader has sexually abused another adult, one has to wonder what God thinks about it. The Bible contains many stories in which God's anger burned against the sin He saw. And at other times, His grace surpassed what anyone could imagine.

Abraham pleaded with God to spare the cities of Sodom and Gomorrah. Even if there were just ten righteous people, would He be willing to spare the city? God said He would, but ten could not be found. Both cities burned with sulfur from heaven. Punishment and justice were served.

Remember the time of Korah, Dathan, and Abiram? Or the story of Achan? God served justice to these men and their families. And there were others. How about God's judgment on Eli, on Israel and Judah, on Solomon, and on Nebuchadnezzar? All of these are reminders that God's righteousness requires justice.

GOD'S GRACE

God is so good to us. We could never count the times He has shown love and mercy and has forgiven us when we don't deserve it.

The Bible shares many stories of God's grace. Remember how Joseph's brothers traded him to a group of traveling Egyptians? Although things weren't good for Joseph for a long time, he later rose to power and was Egypt's second-in-command. God's grace softened Joseph's heart so that he was able to forgive his brothers. What his brothers meant for evil, God turned into good.

Saul hated the church and the followers of The Way. He had plans to arrest them, and the church feared his defying threats. But God had other plans for Saul. By His grace, Saul was called to be one of the greatest leaders of the Bible (and of all time). God's grace saved him.

UNDERSTANDING GOD'S JUSTICE AND GOD'S GRACE

Think about Joseph. He must have spent hours wondering what he had done wrong. He must have blamed himself at times and questioned his own actions and behavior. In prison he must have wondered why God didn't rescue him and get him out of there. Where was God? Why would He allow this to happen? He knew that His God could do anything to change Joseph's circumstances. So where was justice? He was being punished when he had done no wrong.

Or how about Moses? As he changed from being a prince of Egypt to a shepherd in the desert, his thoughts must have gone over the events that were happening to his people in Egypt. Those forty years must have been a time of asking God, *Where are You? Why don't you keep the promises You made to our forefathers? Why do You allow your people to be mistreated?*

Then think about Bathsheba. Many of her days must have been spent in tears. Her losses were unfathomably great—all because a king violated boundaries to have his needs met. Nothing could be done to reverse what had happened. Besides the prophet Nathan, no one dared to question David or hold him accountable for what he had done. She must have cried for justice, but her voice was not heard.

Out of all of this bad, God's grace came to give good. He empowered Moses to do something he did not feel equipped for. He answered Joseph's cry for help by raising him up to be a leader. He brought healing to a broken woman's heart as she was forced to move on with her new life.

God does that. He brings healing and restoration to the broken hearts of his people. Even in the midst of abuse, God's touch and love can help His people work through the impossible, heal their brokenness, and give to them recovery and restoration.

NEVER THE SAME AGAIN...

Joseph, Moses, and Bathsheba were never the same again. The injustices that happened in their lives changed them into persons they never knew they could be. Through prayer and steadfast love for their Father, they took what was bad in their lives and allowed God to transform them into something new. I doubt any of them wanted to go through the hardship they endured—or would choose it again. But because of God's love and grace, their lives were brought back to a renewed self, a restored self, and a transformed self.

The same thing can happen following abuse in the church. After the difficulty has passed, ask God how He can transform what was hurtful and damaging into something good. Implore Him about what He would like you to become so that your experience can bring healing to other lives. Just as Joseph went from living in a dungeon to becoming a prince, trust God to do the same for you. What you never would have imagined you could do may be His call for you.

It's likely that God's grace *and* justice will both be apparent when a church responds to abuse. At times, harshness is not appropriate. And at other times, accountability and punishment will be necessary. Sometimes hearts will soften and the embrace of the Savior will feel real, and then sometimes there will be anger and retaliation for pain so great. One thing is certain for the church that has known abuse: It will never be the same again.

Encounter self

Conflict is a time when God's truth comes to us through three encounters: self, God, and others.[59] Encountering yourself is important. During this time, one needs to seek to understand justice and grace, God's love and God's judgment. Time for yourself means you are willing to reflect on what has happened to you so you will be better able to understand how you were affected by the experience. Time with yourself means you need to slow down your life and be more aware of your thoughts and feelings.

No matter what degree of involvement you have had with abuse by the church, your thoughts will be driven to trying to understand why it happened. Whether you were the perpetrator, a victim, a family member, or a church member, God wants you to wrestle with Him. He wants you on your knees—praying, pleading, crying, and searching Scripture—so that you will again realize that the prevalence of sin in the world and in the church is great and that we must depend on Him solely at all times to fight off Satanic attacks.

In the process of being transformed by a negative church experience, it's important to look deeply inside yourself. Enter a time of greater discipline of reading Scripture and spending time in prayer. Reflect on what changes you need to make so your relationship with God can be strengthened. Ask God to awaken you and show you where you need to grow. Ask Him to reveal to you what needs to be different in your life. Challenge God with questions that don't have easy answers.

Encounter God

By allowing God to speak to you, you will be silencing the angry voices within, thereby making it possible to hear God's voice. By listening intently to what He is saying, you can be assured that you will better understand what He desires as you travel the road to recovery.[60]

We have a great God. He is omnipresent (present everywhere), omniscient (all-knowing), and omnipotent (all-powerful.) He is sovereign and ruler over all. Sometimes we forget about His greatness. Our lives can easily become busy and burdened with schedules, finances, family issues, and fun. We easily become enticed by what the world has to offer, and focusing on God and what He wants in our lives fades away.

So when a hurricane, tornado, or tsunami in the form of church abuse comes into our lives, we are quick to blame anyone for what happened, including God. We ask God, "Why did You allow this? We're good people. Why would You let someone do this? We're not as bad as that other congregation down the road. Now *they* could use something bad happening to them…but not us."

Encountering our great God is what develops maturity, growth, and change in our spirits. Encountering Him is what forces us to *call on* Him, *implore* Him, and *wrestle with* Him. When the very foundation of our lives and our church community has been under attack and we are crumbling and heading for shambles, God is all that is left—and God is all that we need.

When one of your church leaders has abused you or betrayed your church members, when you have been viciously and wrongfully attacked by church administration or they have slandered your name, or when you have been accused of things you never did, seek the face of God. Trust Him even when you think you can't.

Encounter others

We need to hear from others. They have so much to teach us. Listen carefully to what others are trying to tell you about this experience, and use their insights to help you gain in the understanding of what happened.[61]

TRULY TRANSFORMED

Transformation is about encountering: self, God, and others. It is a search that goes deep and long as we redefine ourselves—who we are, what we are doing, and where God and others fit in our lives. Transformation is about looking inward and upward and asking many questions about why this happened. Transformation is about being changed into something we weren't before, and the new "we" must take on a form and shape that is God-fashioned.

Paul says to us, "Do not conform any longer to the pattern of this world, but be transformed by the renewing of your mind. Then you will be able to test and approve what God's will is—his good, pleasing and perfect will" (Romans 12:2–3). And then, "We…are being transformed into his likeness" (1 Corinthians 3:18).

When abuse has happened to you or someone you love, you will be forced to confront the experience whether you want to or not. Sadly, the memories of the hurt and the triggers related to the abuse will not go away. The memories will diminish but will never be forgotten. The abuse experience will come to mind from time to time; the innocence you once knew is no more. Peace is gone because abuse robs every time.

Because we have God and because He is the Great Healer of broken hearts, we live in hope. We live in the hope that we can heal through God's goodness and grace. We can be transformed from someone who is wounded and broken into someone who is made brand new. This transformation is about taking something bad that happened to you and making it into something all new.

Remember the city where suicide was high and morale was low? When hope seemed to be nowhere, God's people called on their God, and a city that was nearly lost was changed into something brand new. He can do the same for those hurt by the church. When a church leader abuses, God can reach down and touch your broken heart, bind up your wounds, and carry you close to His heart, changing you into something brand new.

I know this because He did it for me.

And I know He can do it for you.

Part 5
Persistent for Justice

Voice of the Persistent Widow

The persistent widow struggled with something she couldn't get off her mind: the injustices caused by her adversary. We don't know what those injustices really were—yes, this is a parable—but Jesus had something in mind to teach us about the importance of pursuing justice and granting justice.

It's possible that the widow ruminated, stewed, and even cried about how someone was provoking her, hurting her, or falsely accusing her. Maybe she was faced with harassment, defamation, or even abuse. What we for certain know is that she sought out justice repeatedly because she just couldn't handle the wrongs any longer. And because she wearied him, the judge ultimately granted what she wanted: justice.

The same is true for victims. After being abused by the church, victims approach church leadership with the hopes of being heard. Their hearts are heavy and their minds confused about what has been done to them. Like the persistent widow, they are upset and frustrated and hurt and angry at how they have been victimized and abused by the church.

Yet, at times, their persistence falls on deaf ears.

Could we say that the church today then becomes like the judge in the story? It's possible. Avoidance and denial would be roadblocks that would result in doing nothing. Even a victim's persistence sometimes proves to have limited effect in getting a church to respond. Too many times, our stubborn hearts stand strong, and nothing is done for our victims.

Hear the voice of the persistent widow. Hear the voice of the persistent victim. Their cries for justice and their determination not to enable a system to go slack on what is right and fair is what their message is about. As a church, we must stand ready and willing to hear their voices and respond with justice, just as the judge did.

Our Judge demands nothing less.

Chapter 12
Devote Yourselves to Prayer... and Then Watch

Since, then, you have been raised with Christ, set your hearts on things above,
where Christ is seated at the right hand of God. Set your mind on things
above, not on earthly things. Put to death, therefore, whatever belongs to your
earthly nature: sexual immorality, impurity, lust, evil desires, and greed, which
is idolatry. Because of these, the wrath of God is coming.

Colossians 3:1–2, 5–6

The reality is this: Abuse by a church leader has happened and is happening. There is no denying it. Victims can testify and prove it, councils and congregations can verify it, and lawsuits can show documentation of it. Abuse in the context of the church is real.

DO YOU BELIEVE?

Although statistics show that abuse by pastors and church leaders is higher than we would like it to be (or than we'd even like to *imagine*), why is it so difficult to truly believe that this kind of abuse is happening? Just like it is difficult to acknowledge that we *all* come from dysfunctional families, it is the same with the church. We just don't want to believe that we are that bad! We don't want to entertain the reality that leaders in our denomination and pastors in our church system would do such things. *We're Calvinist; we're Reformed; we're well-indoctrinated; we're good people. It just can't be that our church leaders would abuse.*

That kind of pride and self-righteousness may be a good place to start in trying to understand why abuse is happening within our churches. Denying that we would—or could—ever do such things is a roadblock to really looking within ourselves to see who and what we are really all about. Once we get those blinders off and are willing to face the truth about ourselves, our churches, and our sins, we have positioned ourselves to better know who we are and why we do the things we do. And why abuse happens may even begin make sense.

In the Meantime

There are many in church leadership and church membership who do not believe that abuse within the church is real. They resist hearing about this subject and will openly tell you so if you ask. I've had many of those conversations.

There are several things we can do to address this resistance. First of all, we must pray. We must pray that abuse in the church and by the church will end. We must pray that the churches that are faced with investigating abuse allegations will have the wisdom and guidance and knowledge about what to do and how to do it. We must pray for victims, perpetrators, and their families as they go through a trying time and ask God to provide needed strength. We must be faithful in praying.

Second, we must move forward with what we know. We cannot wait for those who don't understand abuse issues to come around before we do something. With God's help, we must pray that He will open doors of opportunity to address and deal with abuse issues and trust that He will give us strength to withstand the forces when they are against us. We must pray that our testimony through words and actions will influence those who don't believe that abuse is real and that our behavior will be used to help them see it differently.

We must pray that we and others will be willing to learn about abuse and its effects. Insist that your congregation and church council have regular training in what abuse is and how to respond to it. Read books, ask questions, and discuss this topic with your friends. Pray that we will be willing to change and grow in a better understanding of abuse and how to help those who have been affected by it.

Also, we must pray that God would help us advocate for the victim every time. It's easy to pat someone on the back and say, "Yes, I'm praying for you." It's quite another thing to stand in the gap and defend and be the voice for someone who has been abused by the church. Pray that God will empower you to have the courage to stand up for someone who has been abused. Be persistent.

Devote Yourselves to Prayer

Make a list today of all of the people and churches you know that are in a crisis of addressing abuse allegations. Include in your list denominational personnel, classis leaders and pastors, and church councils. Especially pray for victims, perpetrators, and their families as they face unknown futures. Pray that an awakening will happen in your church and faith community. Be persistent in your prayers to God, insisting that justice must prevail.

Paul says, "Devote yourselves to prayer, being watchful and thankful. And pray for us, too, that God may open a door for our message [about abuse by the church]" (Colossians 4:2–3). Because all of our church members need to know.

Bibliography

American Psychiatric Association. *Diagnostic and Statistical Manual of Mental Disorders,* 4th ed., text revision. Washington, DC: American Psychiatric Association, 2000.

Benyei, Candace R. et al. *When a Congregation Is Betrayed: Responding to Clergy Misconduct.* Herndon, VA: The Alban Institute, 2006.

Borgdorff, Peter. *Manual of Christian Reformed Church Government.* 2008 rev. Grand Rapids: Faith Alive Christian Resources, 2008.

Buzzard, Lynn R., and Thomas S. Brandon Jr. *Church Discipline and the Courts,* Wheaton, IL: Tyndale House Publishers, 1987.

Dictionary.com. http://dictionary.reference.com.

Fortune, Marie M., and James N. Poling. *Sexual Abuse by Clergy: A Crisis for the Church.* Decatur, GA: Journal of Pastoral Care Publications, 1996.

Laaser, Mark. *Healing the Wounds of Sexual Addiction.* Grand Rapids: Zondervan, 2004.

Lederach, John Paul. *The Journey Toward Reconciliation.* Scottsdale, PA: Herald Press, 1999.

Life Application Study Bible. Carol Stream, IL: Tyndale House Publishers and Grand Rapids, MI: Zondervan, 2005.

The People's Law Dictionary. http://legal-dictionary.thefreedictionary.com.

"Power And Control Wheel," *Domestic Abuse Intervention Project.* www.theduluthmodel.org/pdf/PhyVio.pdf (accessed 27 June 2010).

Taylor, Thomas F. *Seven Deadly Lawsuits: How Ministers Can Avoid Litigation and Regulation.* Nashville, TN: Abingdon Press, 1996.

VanVonderen, Jeff. *Tired of Trying to Measure Up.* Minneapolis, MN: Bethany House Publishers, 1989.

Endnotes

1. "Power And Control Wheel," *Domestic Abuse Intervention Programs* www.theduluthmodel.org/pdf/PhyVio.pdf (accessed 27 June 2010).

2. Jeff VanVonderen, *Tired of Trying to Measure Up* (Minneapolis, MN: Bethany House Publishers, 1989).

3. Mark Laaser, *Healing the Wounds of Sexual Addiction* (Grand Rapids: Zondervan, 2004).

4. Candace R. Benyei et al., *When a Congregation Is Betrayed: Responding to Clergy Misconduct* (Herndon, VA: The Alban Institute, 2006), 21.

5. Marie M. Fortune and James N. Poling, *Sexual Abuse by Clergy: A Crisis for the Church* (Decatur, GA: Journal of Pastoral Care Publications, 1996), 47.

6. Fortune and Poling, *Sexual Abuse by Clergy*, 7.

7. Ibid., 6–8.

8. "Privileged communication" (n.d.), *The People's Law Dictionary*, http://legal-dictionary.thefreedictionary.com/privileged+communication (accessed 2 August 2009).

9. "Confidential communication" (n.d.), *The People's Law Dictionary*, http://legal-dictionary.thefreedictionary.com/confidential%20communication (accessed 2 August 2009).

10. Lynn R. Buzzard and Thomas S. Brandon Jr., *Church Discipline and the Courts* (Wheaton, IL: Tyndale House Publishers, 1987), 104–5.

11. "Slander" (n.d.), *Dictionary.com*, http://dictionary.reference.com/browse/slander (accessed 2 August 2009).

12. "Libel" (n.d.), *Dictionary.com*, http://dictionary.reference.com/browse/libel (accessed 2 August 2009).

13. Laaser, *Healing the Wounds of Sexual Addiction*, 194.

14. Ibid., 29.

15. Ibid., 30–1.

16. Ibid., 29–30, 33–5.

17. Thomas F. Taylor, *Seven Deadly Lawsuits: How Ministers Can Avoid Litigation and Regulation* (Nashville, TN: Abingdon Press, 1996), 21.

18. Ibid., 21–2.

19. Ibid., 23–4.

20. Ibid., 26.

21. Ibid., 32–3.
22. Ibid., 41.
23. Ibid., 44.
24. Ibid., 51–3.
25. Ibid., 54.
26. Ibid., 78–80.
27. Ibid., 83–4.
28. Ibid., 84.
29. Ibid., 84.
30. Ibid., 108–9.
31. Ibid., 110–1.
32. Ibid., 120.
33. Ibid., 121.
34. Ibid., 121–9.
35. Ibid., 135–6.
36. Benyei et al., *When a Congregation Is Betrayed*, 3.
37. Ibid., 3.
38. Fortune and Poling, *Sexual Abuse by Clergy*, 9–10.
39. Ibid.
40. Ibid., 12.
41. Ibid., 12.
42. Peter Borgdorff, *Manual of Christian Reformed Church Government* (Grand Rapids: Faith Alive Christian Resources, 2008).
43. Ibid.
44. Ibid.
45. Ibid.
46. Benyei et al., *When a Congregation Is Betrayed*.
47. Ibid.
48. Borgdorff, *Manual of Christian Reformed Church Government*.
49. Ibid.
50. Benyei et al., *When a Congregation Is Betrayed*.
51. Borgdorff, *Manual of Christian Reformed Church Government*.
52. Ibid.
53. Ibid.
54. Ibid.
55. Benyei et al., *When a Congregation Is Betrayed*.
56. Ibid.
57. Ibid., 57.
58. Ibid., 57.
59. John Paul Lederach, *The Journey Toward Reconciliation* (Scottsdale, PA: Herald Press, 1999).
60. Ibid.
61. Ibid.

About the Author

Judy De Wit grew up the youngest of five kids near a small town in northwest Iowa and is a lifelong member of the Christian Reformed Church. She graduated from Dordt College in 1984 and taught in Christian schools for fourteen years. In 1999, she received her MA in Marriage and Family Therapy from North American Baptist Seminary and became a licensed therapist a short time later. She also is a graduate of Bethel Seminary and has an MA in Theological Studies with an emphasis in Pastoral Care and Counseling. She is currently a student at Northwestern College of Roseville, MN, studying leadership within the church or nonprofit.

Judy works as a therapist in the Twins Cities Metro area. She served as a cochair for the Abuse Response Team for Classis Lake Superior for three years, is trained in victim advocacy by the Minnesota Council of Churches, and serves as an advocate for victims of church leadership abuse within the Christian Reformed Church. Judy has done numerous abuse trainings for churches and staff, has spoken in churches about abuse, and writes a quarterly newsletter regarding the subject of abuse. She served as an advocate for the Wesley Heersink case, one of the biggest abuse cases that had gone through the CRC denomination. Visit her Web site at www.abuseministries.org for more information.

Outside of work, Judy enjoys flowers, walking, writing, playing the piano, and watching Twins Baseball and is an avid fan of NFL football.